GROWING FRUIT TREES FOR
BEGINNERS

Grow delicious fruit naturally in USDA Zones 6–8. A hands-on guide for small gardens, home orchards, and a more self-sufficient, rewarding lifestyle

Sienna Greenfell

Verdora Press

Grow with Nature. Live in Harmony

TABLE OF CONTENTS

INTRODUCTION... 7

CHAPTER 1... 10

KNOW YOUR GROWING ZONE.. 10

    Understanding Your USDA Hardiness Zone 10

    Design Your Home Orchard for Success 12

    Preparing Your Soil Naturally...................................... 18

    Grafting Made Simple 27

    Smart Watering for a Healthy Orchard 31

    Natural Pest & Disease Control.................................... 33

    Avoid the Top 10 Orchard Mistakes.............................. 38

CHAPTER 2... 42

GROWING IN USDA ZONE 6... 42

    The Opportunities in Zone 6 44

    Best Fruit Trees and Berries for Cold Climates 45

    Winter and Frost Protection.. 48

    Annual Irrigation and Care Program 52

    Permaculture for Cold Climates................................... 55

    Annual Orchard Care Calendar.................................... 58

CHAPTER 3... 61

GROWING IN USDA ZONE 7... 61

    Zone 7 Climate: 62

    Maximizing Growth and Fruit Production...................... 67

    Applying Permaculture in Mixed Climates 74

    Annual Orchard Care Calendar.................................... 78

CHAPTER 4... 82

GROWING IN USDA ZONE 8....................................82

Zone 8 Climate...83

Subtropical Fruit Trees.......................................86

Summer Care & Water Conservation.............................89

Selecting Low-Chill Fruit Varieties 92

Summer Pest & Disease Control, Naturally 94

Applying Permaculture in Hot Climates 98

Annual Orchard Care Calendar 101

CONCLUSION 105

INTRODUCTION

Growing an orchard is much more than simply planting a few trees: it's an act of trust in nature, a concrete step toward building health, beauty, and self-sufficiency in your own corner of the world.

If you're reading these pages, chances are you feel the desire to harvest real fruit straight from your land, to fill your pantry with authentic flavors, and to reconnect more deeply with the earth.

It doesn't matter whether you have a large field, a family garden, or just a small backyard— with the right strategies, anyone can create a thriving, lasting orchard.

This book was written with you in mind: for those who seek clear, simple, and effective solutions, without getting lost in complicated technical jargon. My goal is to guide you step by step—from selecting the right trees to enjoying abundant harvests—with methods tailored to the climates of USDA Zones 6,

7, and 8.

Why these three zones together?

Zones 6, 7, and 8 share many common challenges—and by understanding the full range, you'll be better prepared to adapt, adjust, and succeed, no matter what your specific microclimate brings.

Plus, weather patterns are changing.

Growing knowledge across neighboring zones gives you more tools, more options, and more confidence to build a resilient, thriving orchard for years to come.

Inside these pages, you'll find:

- Practical, natural techniques for growing fruit trees and berries with real, lasting results
- Targeted strategies to overcome the unique climate challenges of your zone
- Permaculture-inspired advice to create a healthy, resilient, and eco-friendly orchard
- Easy-to-follow tables, checklists, and calendars to organize each step effortlessly

This book is designed to be modular:

In **Part 1**, you'll discover the universal foundations every successful orchard needs.

Starting from **Part 2**, you can dive into specific strategies tailored for your climate: Zones 6, 7, or 8.

At the beginning, you'll find a practical guide to help you quickly locate the sections most relevant to you.

Your orchard won't grow overnight, but with the right tools and a clear guide, each season will bring you closer to a generous and rewarding harvest.

Are you ready to set down deep roots and reap the rewards of your hard work?

How to Use This Book

This book is divided into two main parts:

Part 1: Universal Foundations

Learn the essential techniques for planting, caring for, and sustaining a healthy orchard, no matter your USDA zone.

Parts 2, 3, and 4: Zone-Specific Strategies

Find detailed guidance adapted to your local climate:

- **Zone 6** growers: start with Part 2.
- **Zone 7** growers: go to Part 3.
- **Zone 8** growers: jump to Part 4.

If you already know your zone, feel free to go directly to your section.

If you're unsure, check the USDA Zone Finder at the beginning of this book.

Inside your section, you'll find:

- Recommended fruit trees and berries
- Seasonal care calendars
- Climate-specific challenges and solutions
- Practical permaculture techniques

Tip: Exploring other zones can offer extra insights and ideas to strengthen your orchard's resilience.

Chapter 1

KNOW YOUR GROWING ZONE

Understanding Your USDA Hardiness Zone

Before you plant anything, it's important to understand *where* you're growing.

Every location has a different climate—and fruit trees love consistency.

Choosing the right trees for your zone means fewer problems, stronger plants, and better harvests.

The USDA (United States Department of Agriculture) created a map that divides the U.S. into **"hardiness zones"** based on the **coldest temperatures each area usually gets in winter.**

This book focuses on three popular home-growing zones:

- **Zone 6** (cold winters, short growing season)
- **Zone 7** (mild winters, longer season)
- **Zone 8** (mild to warm winters, long season)

What Exactly Is a USDA Zone?

Each zone is based on the *average* minimum winter temperature:

- **Zone 6:** –10°F to 0°F (–23°C to –18°C)
- **Zone 7:** 0°F to 10°F (–18°C to –12°C)
- **Zone 8:** 10°F to 20°F (–12°C to –6°C)

These numbers help you understand:

- What fruit trees can survive your winters
- How long your growing season will be
- How much cold your plants will experience each year

How to Find Your Zone (It's Easy!)

Here's how to find your exact USDA zone in less than a minute:

1. Go to https://planthardiness.ars.usda.gov/
2. Type in your ZIP code
3. Your zone will appear instantly

You can also check maps online or ask at your local garden center—they almost always know!

Why It Matters for Your Fruit Trees

Imagine this:

You plant a peach tree that needs warm weather, but you live in Zone 6 where winters are harsh. That tree might *never* produce fruit—or worse, it might not survive the winter.

Knowing your zone helps you:

- Choose trees that will thrive, not just survive
- Avoid wasting money and time
- Plan your planting and harvesting better

Quick Zone Summary

Zone	Climate Summary	Typical Growing Season
Zone 6	Cold winters, late spring frosts	May to mid-October
Zone 7	Milder winters, balanced seasons	April to late October
Zone 8	Warm winters, early springs	March to November

You might notice your local weather feels a little warmer or colder than what your USDA zone suggests.

That's okay! Things like **elevation, wind, shade, and nearby bodies of water** create *microclimates* in your yard.

In Part 1 of this book, you'll learn how to work with your own space—no matter the zone—by using smart planning and simple natural techniques. Now that you know your zone, let's start building your orchard the right way—one simple step at a tim.

Design Your Home Orchard for Success

Starting a fruit orchard doesn't mean you need a huge piece of land. Even a small backyard—or a sunny side yard—can become a productive, beautiful space with the right plan.

Before planting anything, it's important to take a step back and **design your orchard on paper**. A smart layout will save you time, money, and frustration down the road.

Let's break it down into three steps:

1. How Much Space Do You Really Need?

The first question most beginners ask is:

"How many trees should I plant?"

Here's the good news: even just **3–5 well-chosen trees** can provide **baskets of fruit** every season.

Here's a general guide:

Tree Type	Spacing Needed	Typical Yield
Dwarf Tree	8–10 feet (2.5–3 m) apart	1–2 bushels/year
Semi-Dwarf Tree	12–15 feet (3.5–4.5 m) apart	3–6 bushels/year
Standard Tree	18–25 feet (5.5–7.5 m) apart	5–10 bushels/year

Choose **dwarf or semi-dwarf** trees if you have limited space. They're easier to manage, prune, and harvest—perfect for home growers.

2. Planning the Layout

Think of your orchard like a mini ecosystem. You want:

- **Good airflow** (to prevent disease)
- **Plenty of sunlight** (at least 6–8 hours/day)
- **Easy access for watering, pruning, and harvesting**

Here's a simple layout tip:

- Place **taller trees** on the **north or west side** of your space
- Plant **smaller trees or berry bushes** to the **south or east**, where they won't be shaded

You can also **create rows** with walking paths in between, or plant in **clusters** (guilds) if you're following permaculture principles.

3. How Many Varieties Do You Need?

It depends on what you want:

- **Do you want fruit all season long?** → Choose early, mid, and late varieties
- **Want to preserve fruit?** → Choose high-yield types like apple, pear,

or plum

- **Want variety?** → Mix trees (one apple, one pear, one peach, etc.)

Most fruit trees need to be **pollinated** by another variety that blooms at the same time.

For example:

- Apples need a second apple variety nearby (e.g., 'Fuji' + 'Granny Smith')
- Blueberries of different varieties help each other produce more

Don't worry—later in the book you'll find **charts that show exactly which varieties work together.**

Example: Small Orchard Plan for a Family

Let's say you have 20 x 30 feet (6 x 9 meters) of sunny space. You could fit:

- 3 semi-dwarf trees (apple, pear, peach)
- 4–6 berry bushes (blueberries, raspberries, blackberries)
- A few herbs and pollinator flowers around the base

With this setup, you could harvest fresh fruit from **June to October**, and still have space to move around, mulch, water, and enjoy the view.

Tips Before You Sketch Your Orchard

- Start small. It's better to **plant fewer trees and care for them well** than to overplant and feel overwhelmed.
- Leave space to expand later—once you fall in love with growing fruit, you'll want to add more!
- Always think **sunlight, airflow, water access**, and **pollination partners.**

Permaculture for a Healthy Orchard

Permaculture might sound like a big, complicated word—

but it simply means **working with nature**, not against it.

In this chapter, you'll learn a few easy ways to design your orchard so it becomes **more productive, more resilient**, and much easier to manage over time.

Let's keep it simple and focus on three key ideas.

1. Natural Design: Let the Land Guide You

Instead of forcing a perfect grid of trees, permaculture encourages you to **observe your space first**:

- Where does the sun hit the longest?
- Where does water collect after rain?
- Which parts are windy, shaded, or protected?

Simple tip:

Spend a few days just watching your garden.

Notice how sunlight moves, where puddles form, and where the soil stays dry.

Then, **plant accordingly**:

- Put sun-loving trees in the brightest spots
- Use naturally shaded areas for berries or companion plants
- Place hardy trees or shrubs where winds are stronger

This approach saves time and water—because you're working with your land's natural flow.

2. Smart Water Management

One of the best permaculture tricks is to **slow down and keep water where you need it**, especially during hot or dry months.

Here's how to do that:

Mulching:

Cover the soil around your trees and berry bushes with straw, leaves, wood chips, or dried grass.

This keeps the soil moist longer, blocks weeds, and feeds the soil as it breaks down.

Swales:

If your land is slightly sloped, you can dig small, shallow ditches—called **swales**—along contour lines.

These catch rainwater and **let it soak into the ground** instead of running off.

Rain Catchment:

Place a barrel under your gutter or roof edge. You'll be surprised how much free water you can collect—even from a light rain!

3. Build a Biodiversity-Friendly Orchard

The more **living variety** you invite into your orchard, the better it will perform—naturally. Here's how:

Add flowers and herbs:

Plant lavender, comfrey, calendula, mint, and other low-maintenance herbs around your trees.

They attract bees, ladybugs, and other beneficial insects—and they're beautiful!

Encourage beneficial bugs:

Let go of the idea that every bug is a problem.

Ladybugs, lacewings, and certain wasps **help control pests** naturally.

You can attract them with flowering plants, rock piles, or even small insect "hotels."

Include support plants:

In permaculture, we often use **"guilds"**—small communities of plants that work together.

For example, under an apple tree, you might plant:

- **Chives** (repel pests)
- **Dandelions** (pull nutrients from deep soil)
- **Clover** (adds nitrogen to the soil)

This system strengthens your orchard without needing chemicals.

What Makes a Permaculture Orchard Special?

- It **saves water**, energy, and effort
- It **gets stronger every season**
- It becomes a place full of life—not just trees and fruit, but birds, bees, flowers, and healthy soil

You don't need to apply every principle at once.

Start small: maybe add mulch, plant one beneficial flower, or try catching rainwater.

Each step builds a more balanced system.

Now that you understand how to design your orchard *with* nature, it's time to prepare the soil—the foundation of everything.

Next, we'll walk through how to test, enrich, and care for your soil naturally, so your trees and berries have the best possible start.

Preparing Your Soil Naturally

Good soil is the real secret behind strong, healthy fruit trees.

You can choose the best tree varieties and have the perfect sunny spot—but if your soil isn't right, your orchard will struggle.

The good news?

You don't need expensive fertilizers or complicated chemical treatments.

A few simple steps can transform your soil into a rich, living foundation that your trees and berries will love.

Let's walk through the three essentials:

1. Step One: Test Your Soil

Before planting anything, it's important to **understand what you're working with**.

Here's what you want to find out:

- **Soil texture** (Is it sandy, clay, loamy?)
- **Soil pH** (Is it acidic, neutral, or alkaline?)
- **Organic matter** (Is the soil rich and dark, or pale and lifeless?)

How to test your soil easily:

- **Texture test:**

  Grab a handful of moist soil and squeeze it.

  - If it crumbles, it's sandy.
  - If it stays tight and sticky, it's clay.
  - If it forms a ball but breaks apart easily, it's loam (perfect!).

- **pH test:**

  You can buy an inexpensive soil pH test kit online or at garden centers.

  Fruit trees generally prefer a **slightly acidic to neutral pH** (between 6.0 and 7.0).

- **Organic matter check**:

Healthy soil looks dark, crumbles easily, and smells slightly sweet.

If your soil is too acidic or alkaline, don't worry. We'll cover easy fixes in the next section.

2. Step Two: Improve Your Soil Naturally

You don't need chemicals to fix your soil—you just need **to feed it like nature does**. Here's how:

Add organic matter: mix compost, aged manure, shredded leaves, or grass clippings into the soil.

This improves texture, balances nutrients, and boosts life underground.

Use mulch: cover the soil with a thick layer (2–4 inches) of mulch around your trees and bushes.

- Mulch keeps the soil moist
- Protects roots from temperature swings
- Slowly adds nutrients as it breaks down

Good mulches: straw, wood chips, pine needles, shredded leaves.

Fix pH naturally

- If soil is **too acidic** (below 6.0): add **garden lime** slowly over time.
- If soil is **too alkaline** (above 7.5): add **elemental sulfur** or lots of organic matter.

Always retest after a few months to track progress.

3. Step Three: Compost — Your Orchard's Best Friend

Compost is pure magic for fruit trees and berries.

It's easy to make, costs almost nothing, and creates a steady supply of rich nutrients.

What you can compost:

- Fruit and vegetable scraps
- Coffee grounds and tea bags

- Grass clippings, leaves, and small branches
- Eggshells (crushed)

What you should NOT compost:

- Meat, dairy, oily foods (they attract pests)
- Diseased plants

Simple beginner method:

- Pile organic waste in a bin or open corner
- Turn it with a shovel once a week to let it breathe
- Keep it moist but not soaking wet
- After 2–6 months, you'll have dark, crumbly compost ready to use!

Apply compost around the base of trees and bushes to **feed the soil naturally** year after year.

Quick Checklist:

1. Test soil texture and Ph
2. Add organic matter (compost, mulch, leaves)
3. Correct pH if needed
4. Start a compost pile for long-term soil health

By preparing your soil naturally, you're not just planting trees—you're building a living, breathing foundation for a healthy orchard that will thrive for decades. In the next chapter, we'll talk about how to **choose the best trees and berries** for your land, your climate, and your family's goals.

Choosing the Right Fruit Trees and Berries

Choosing the right trees and berries is one of the most exciting parts of building your orchard.

But it's also one of the most important decisions—because planting the wrong varieties for your climate can mean years of poor harvests or tree struggles.

Let's make sure you pick winners from the start.

1. Prioritize Local and Proven Varieties

Whenever possible, choose fruit trees and berries that are **well adapted to your region**.

Local or regional varieties are:

- More resistant to common pests and diseases
- Better adapted to local rainfall, soil, and temperatures
- More reliable producers, even in challenging seasons

Where to find the best information:

- Local nurseries and garden centers
- County extension offices
- Regional fruit tree grower associations
- Farmers' markets (ask growers what varieties they plant!)

If a tree or berry is thriving in your neighbor's yard, it will likely thrive in yours too.

2. Choose Hardy and Disease-Resistant Varieties

Some fruit trees are naturally tougher than others.

As a beginner, it's smart to choose **varieties bred for disease resistance and cold or heat tolerance**, depending on your USDA zone.

For example:

- **Apples**: 'Liberty', 'Enterprise', and 'Freedom' resist common diseases like apple scab and fire blight.

- **Pears**: 'Kieffer' and 'Moonglow' are tough and disease-resistant.
- **Peaches**: 'Reliance' (great for cold zones) or 'Florida Prince' (great for warm zones).
- **Berries**: Modern varieties like 'Heritage' raspberries and 'Sunshine Blue' blueberries are strong producers with minimal care.

Choosing hardy varieties means:

- Fewer pests
- Less need for chemical sprays
- Higher success even if your weather is unpredictable

3. Plan for a Long Harvest Season

One of the best orchard secrets?

Grow varieties that ripen at different times, so you enjoy fresh fruit for months instead of just a few weeks.

This is called seasonal succession, and it's easy to plan:

Fruit Type	Early Season	Mid Season	Late Season
Apples	Lodi	Liberty	Enterprise
Peaches	Desiree	Redhaven	Encore
Pears	Harrow Delight	Bartlett	Seckel
Blueberries	Duke	Bluecrop	Elliott
Raspberries	Polka	Heritage	Caroline

By mixing early, mid, and late varieties, you'll enjoy fruit from **June to October** in most climates!

Quick Checklist:

1. Focus on varieties recommended for your zone
2. Look for disease resistance and climate toughness
3. Mix early, mid, and late varieties for a longer harvest
4. Buy trees and plants from reputable, local sources whenever possible

By picking the right trees and berries now, you're setting up your orchard for healthier growth, fewer problems, and delicious rewards for years to come.

In the next section, we'll dive into **how to plant your trees and berries correctly**—because even the best variety needs the right start to thrive.

Planting Tips for a Strong Orchard Start

Once you've chosen your trees and berries, it's time for the most important action: planting them the right way.

A strong start in the ground means faster growth, healthier roots, and earlier fruit production.

Luckily, planting isn't complicated—if you follow a few simple, proven steps. Here's exactly how to do it:

1. When to Plant

The best time to plant is:

- **In early spring** (as soon as the ground is workable)
- **Or in early fall** (at least 4–6 weeks before your first hard frost)

Why? Cooler temperatures and moist soil **reduce transplant shock** and help roots establish quickly.

2. How to Plant Trees and Berries Step-by-Step

Step 1: Choose the Right Spot

- Full sun (6–8 hours minimum)
- Well-drained soil (no puddles after rain)
- Protection from strong winds, if possible

Step 2: Dig a Proper Hole

- Make it **twice as wide** as the root ball, but **no deeper**
- Loosen the soil at the bottom with a fork or shovel

Why? Wide holes encourage roots to spread out easily, leading to a stronger tree.

Step 3: Prepare the Tree or Bush

- Remove the plant gently from its container or wrapping
- If roots are tightly wound ("root-bound"), gently loosen them by hand

Step 4: Set the Plant at the Correct Depth

- **For trees:** The top of the root flare (where the roots start to spread) should be level with the ground surface
- **For berries:** Plant so the soil level matches where it was in the container

Never plant too deep! It can suffocate the roots.

Step 5: Backfill Carefully

- Fill the hole halfway with the original soil
- Water deeply to settle the soil
- Fill the rest of the hole, gently firming it down (no stomping!)

Step 6: Water Thoroughly

- After planting, give your new plant a **slow, deep watering**
- Continue watering regularly (about once or twice a week, depending on weather) for the first full growing season

3. Mulch to Protect and Feed

After planting, apply a 2–4 inch (5–10 cm) layer of mulch around the base, but:

- **Keep mulch 2–4 inches away** from the trunk or main stem
- Mulch touching the trunk can cause rot

Good mulch materials:

- Wood chips
- Straw
- Shredded leaves

Mulch:

- Keeps soil moist
- Regulates soil temperature
- Suppresses weeds
- Adds organic matter as it breaks down

4. Protect Young Plants

Newly planted trees and berries are vulnerable to:

- **Wind damage**

- **Animal browsing** (deer, rabbits)
- **Strong sun or unexpected frost**

Simple protection ideas:

- Use small tree guards or chicken wire around young trunks
- Shade cloth or row covers for sun or frost extremes (especially first year)

Quick Checklist:

1. Choose a sunny, well-drained spot
2. Dig a wide, shallow hole
3. Set the tree at the correct height
4. Water deeply right after planting
5. Mulch carefully but keep it off the trunk
6. Protect from pests and extreme weather

Planting your trees and berries the right way is like **setting a strong foundation for a house**:

Everything you do afterward will be easier and more rewarding if you start right.

Grafting Made Simple

Why Learn to Graft?

Have you ever wished you could harvest different fruit varieties from the same tree? Or save a beloved branch from an old tree that produced amazing fruit? With grafting, all of this becomes possible.

Grafting is a simple, natural technique that allows you to **combine two trees into one**: a branch (called the scion) is joined to a host tree (the rootstock), creating a stronger, more productive plant—perfect for small spaces and personalized orchards.

You don't need to be an expert or have a professional orchard. With curiosity, patience, and a few basic tools, anyone can start grafting.

In this chapter, you'll learn **when, how, and why to graft**, with beginner-friendly, step-by-step instructions.

What You Should Know Before Getting Started

Key Terms:

- **Scion:** The healthy branch or bud from the fruit variety you want to grow.
- **Rootstock:** The base tree that provides roots and structure.
- The **cambium layer** (the green tissue under the bark) of both scion and rootstock must **align closely** for the graft to succeed.

Best Time to Graft in USDA Zones 6–8

- **Spring (March–May):** Ideal for cleft or whip grafting.
- **Summer (July–August):** Great for bud grafting (T-budding).
- Avoid extreme heat or cold—choose mild, dry days.

What You'll Need

- Sharp grafting knife
- Grafting tape or parafilm
- Grafting sealant (optional but helpful)
- Gloves and alcohol to disinfect tools

Beginner-Friendly Grafting Techniques

1. Cleft Graft

- Cut the rootstock straight across (about 2–5 cm in diameter).
- Make a vertical split in the center and insert the wedge-shaped scion.
- Wrap with tape and cover with sealant.
- ➤ Best for dormant fruit trees in early spring.

2. T-Budding (Bud Graft)

- Cut a single healthy bud with a thin slice of bark.
- Make a "T" cut in the bark of the rootstock, lift the flaps, and insert the bud.
- Secure with tape.
- ➤ Perfect for summer grafting.

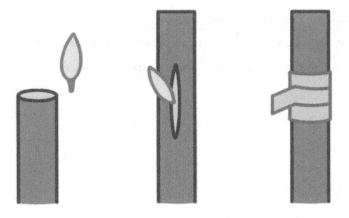

Best Tree Types and Compatibility for USDA Zones 6–8

- **Compatibility is key:** Apple to apple, pear to pear, plum to plum.
- Common combinations:
    - **Apple:** on M9 or MM106 (dwarf or semi-dwarf)
    - **Pear:** on quince or Pyrus communis
    - **Peach/apricot:** on Myrobalan plum or seed-grown peach

Tips for Success

- Use **fresh, healthy scions** from this year's growth
- Always disinfect tools before use
- Protect the graft from wind, direct sun, and pests
- Remove any shoots (suckers) below the graft point

Why Grafting Is Worth It

Grafting allows you to:

- Grow multiple varieties on a single tree
- Save space in your orchard or garden
- Speed up fruit production
- Preserve rare or heirloom varieties

In the next section, we'll explore **how to water and care for your young orchard** through the seasons, using smart, simple methods that support strong, natural growth.

Smart Watering for a Healthy Orchard

Watering may seem simple—but **how** and **when** you water can make a big difference between weak, struggling trees and strong, fruit-filled branches.

No matter your USDA zone, smart watering helps:

- Reduce plant stress
- Prevent disease
- Save time and money
- Build deeper, healthier root systems

Let's explore three beginner-friendly strategies that work in **every zone**.

1. Use Drip Irrigation for Deep, Efficient Watering

Drip irrigation delivers water slowly and directly to the roots, where it's needed most.

Why it works:

- Minimizes waste from evaporation
- Keeps leaves dry (reducing fungal disease)
- Encourages deep root growth
- Can be automated with a timer

What you need:

- A drip hose or tubing with emitters
- A basic connector to your garden faucet
- (Optional) A timer to set watering days and duration

Start small—just run drip lines to your fruit trees and berry bushes. Expand later as needed.

How often should you water?

- **Newly planted trees:** 1–2 times per week for the first year
- **Established trees:** Deep soak every 10–14 days during dry periods
- **Berries:** Light watering 2–3 times a week in hot weather

Always check the soil: if it's damp 2 inches below the surface, you're doing it right.

2. Collect Rainwater and Store It for Free

Rain is free—and plants love it.

Installing a **simple rain catchment system** is a great way to reduce your water bill and prepare for dry weeks.

What you need:

- A rain barrel or food-grade drum
- A screen to block leaves and insects
- A downspout diverter from your roof

One small roof (10x10 ft) can collect over **60 gallons** of water from just **1 inch** of rainfall!

Use the stored water:

- To fill your drip system
- For spot-watering young plants
- During watering restrictions or droughts

Place barrels slightly uphill or use a gravity-fed hose to make distribution easier.

3. Reduce Evaporation and Keep Soil Moist

Watering is only half the battle—**keeping moisture in the soil** is just as important.

Here's how:

Mulch, mulch, mulch

Apply 2–4 inches of mulch around each tree or bush:

- Blocks sun from drying the soil
- Slows water evaporation
- Protects roots from heat and cold

Water in the early morning or evening

Avoid watering in the middle of the day, when sun and heat cause fast evaporation.

Use shade wisely

- In hot zones (Zone 8), consider planting **living shade** like low shrubs or tall grasses on the south side of sensitive plants.
- You can also use temporary **shade cloth** during extreme heat waves.

Quick Checklist:

1. Use drip irrigation for deep, targeted watering
2. Collect rainwater to save and reuse naturally
3. Mulch generously to trap moisture and protect roots
4. Water early or late in the day
5. Check soil before watering to avoid over- or under-watering

With these simple strategies, you'll give your fruit trees and berries exactly what they need—**without wasting a drop**.

In the next section, we'll look at how to keep your orchard naturally healthy by **preventing pests and diseases using nature itself.**

Natural Pest & Disease Control

A thriving orchard isn't just about robust trees; it's about fostering a balanced ecosystem. Instead of relying on chemical pesticides, you can employ natural methods to protect your plants and support the environment simultaneously.

Here's how:

1. Beneficial Insects: Nature's Allies

Certain insects are invaluable allies in the orchard, preying on harmful pests like aphids, mites, and caterpillars.

Common beneficial insects:

- **Ladybugs**: Consume aphids and scale insects.
- **Lacewings**: Their larvae feed on aphids, mites, and insect eggs.
- **Hoverflies**: Larvae eat pests; adults pollinate flowers.

- **Parasitic wasps**: Lay eggs inside pests, halting their reproduction.

How to attract them:

- Plant flowers such as marigolds, fennel, coriander, and nasturtiums.
- Avoid chemical sprays that can harm beneficial insects.
- Create insect-friendly habitats with rocks, logs, or insect hotels.

2. Natural Oils: Safe and Effective Defense

Plant-based oils can protect your orchard from pests without harming humans or pollinators.

Neem Oil:

- Derived from neem tree seeds.
- Controls aphids, whiteflies, mites, and scale insects.
- Disrupts pest feeding and reproduction.
- Safe for pets, humans, and beneficial insects when used correctly .

Canola Oil (Horticultural Oil):

- Coats and suffocates soft-bodied pests.
- Effective against various insect life stages.

Usage Tips:

- Follow product instructions for dilution.
- Apply in the early morning or late afternoon to avoid harming pollinators.
- Reapply every 7–10 days during infestations.

3. Organic Prevention: The Best Defense

Preventing problems before they start is key.

Companion Planting

- **Nasturtiums**: Attract aphids away from fruit trees .
- **Marigolds**: Repel soil pests and nematodes.

Herbal Sprays

- **Nettle Tea**: Strengthens plant defenses and repels aphids.
- **Garlic Spray**: Offers antifungal and antibacterial properties.

Crop Rotation and Diversity

- Mixing plants and rotating crops near fruit trees disrupts pest cycles and confuses insects.

Regular Monitoring

- Inspect your orchard every few days.
- Check leaf undersides and growing tips.
- Address issues early to prevent spread.

Quick Checklist:

1. Attract beneficial insects with flowers and shelters.
2. Use natural oils like neem and canola during outbreaks.
3. Apply homemade teas (e.g., nettle or garlic) preventively.
4. Plant companion species to deter pests.
5. Regularly inspect your orchard for signs of trouble.

By embracing these gentle yet effective techniques, your orchard will become a resilient, self-sustaining system—vibrant and less reliant on synthetic sprays.

Next, we'll explore how to keep your trees productive year-round with a straightforward, seasonal orchard care plan.

Building a Resilient, Fertile Ecosystem

With a little planning, you can turn it into a **living ecosystem**—full of life, balance, and natural protection.

A diverse, healthy environment doesn't just look beautiful—it helps your plants grow better, resist stress, and produce more fruit.

Here are three simple ways to build an orchard that works *with* nature instead of against it.

1. Plant Flowers That Attract Pollinators

Pollinators like bees, butterflies, and hoverflies are **essential** for fruit production. Without them, your trees may bloom but never bear fruit.

To attract them:

- Plant flowers with **bright colors** and **open shapes**
- Choose **native wildflowers** when possible—they thrive with less care and attract local pollinators

Top pollinator-friendly flowers:

- Lavender
- Calendula
- Echinacea (coneflower)
- Borage
- Yarrow
- Bee balm
- Sunflowers

Tip: Cluster flowers to attract more pollinators.

2. Create Habitats for "Good Bugs"

Not all bugs are bad!

Some insects—like ladybugs, lacewings, and parasitic wasps—are natural pest controllers.

Others—like native bees—are powerful pollinators.

Help them settle into your orchard by creating simple homes:

How to do it:

- Leave **logs or rock piles** at the edge of your growing area
- Build or buy a **bug hotel** (a small wooden frame filled with holes, sticks, and straw)
- Avoid using broad-spectrum pesticides that kill good and bad insects alike

The more beneficial insects you attract, the less you'll need to manage pests manually.

3. Use Companion Planting (Fruit Tree Guilds)

In permaculture, a **guild** is a group of plants that support each other. Instead of planting your tree alone, you surround it with companions that:

- Fix nitrogen
- Attract pollinators
- Deter pests
- Break up hard soil
- Provide ground cover to hold moisture

Example: Apple Tree Guild

- **Main Tree**: Apple
- **Pollinator Attractors**: Yarrow, lavender
- **Pest Deterrents**: Chives, garlic
- **Ground Cover**: White clover (adds nitrogen)
- **Dynamic Accumulator**: Comfrey (brings up nutrients from deep soil)

You don't need to be perfect—just start with 2–3 companion plants under each tree, and expand over time.

Quick Checklist:

1. Plant pollinator-friendly flowers near trees and berries
2. Provide shelter for beneficial insects (logs, bug hotels, rock piles)
3. Use companion planting to protect and enrich the soil
4. Limit pesticides that harm helpful insects
5. Observe your space and let nature guide your design

When your orchard becomes a living ecosystem, it works **with you**, not against you.

You'll spend less time fighting pests or fixing problems—and more time harvesting healthy, delicious fruit.

In the next section, we'll explore the most common beginner mistakes—and how to avoid them before they cost you time and effort.

Avoid the Top 10 Orchard Mistakes

Everyone makes mistakes when starting a fruit orchard—and that's okay. But some errors can cost you time, money, and years of fruitless effort. Here are the **10 most common beginner mistakes**, and how to avoid them from day one.

1. Planting Too Deep: planting trees too far into the ground suffocates roots and causes rot.

> ➤ Fix: Keep the root flare **at ground level**, never buried.

2. Overwatering or Underwatering: too much water = root rot. Too little = stress and stunted growth.

> ➤ Fix: Check the soil 2 inches deep before watering. Adjust with the season.

3. Skipping the Soil Test: ignoring your soil means guessing—bad idea.

> ➤ Fix: Test texture and pH. Add compost and organic matter before planting.

4. Choosing the Wrong Variety: wrong zone, wrong fruit. Trees may survive, but won't thrive.

> ➤ Fix: Choose varieties that match your USDA zone and resist local pests.

5. Forgetting About Pollination: some trees need a partner to produce fruit.

> ➤ Fix: Check if your tree is **self-fertile** or needs a **cross-pollinator**.

6. Improper Mulching: no mulch = dry roots and weeds. But mulch against the trunk causes rot.

> ➤ Fix: Apply 2–4 inches of mulch, but keep it **away from the trunk**.

7. Neglecting Pruning: never pruning = weak structure and poor airflow. Over-pruning = stress.

> ➤ Fix: Prune lightly in winter. Focus on dead wood and good shape.

8. Expecting Fruit Too Soon: young trees take time. Impatience leads to frustration.

> ➤ Fix: Focus on root health. Fruit comes in year 2–4 (sometimes later for berries).

9. Using Chemical Sprays Too Soon: panic spraying can kill beneficial insects and weaken your orchard.

> ➤ Fix: Learn natural prevention first (see Section **Natural Techniques for Pest and Disease Control**), and spray only if truly needed.

10. Planting Without a Plan: putting trees "where they fit" leads to shading, crowding, and pollination problems.

> ➤ Fix: Sketch a simple layout. Think: sunlight, spacing, air, water, and access.

Top 3 Mistakes to Double-Check Before Planting
- Is your tree planted too deep?
- Did you test your soil first?
- Did you choose the right variety for your zone and pollination needs?

Fixing these **before you even dig a hole** can save you years of struggle.

With these mistakes behind you, you're now better prepared than most new growers.

In the next section, we'll look at how to keep a simple **orchard diary**—an easy tool to help you stay organized and improve season after season.

Orchard Diary

Even with the best planting and planning, your orchard will teach you something new every year.

That's why keeping a simple **orchard diary** is one of the smartest things a grower can do—especially in the beginning.

It doesn't need to be fancy or time-consuming.

It just needs to be consistent.

What to Record in Your Orchard Diary

Here are a few useful things to jot down throughout the year:

- **Date of planting** for each tree or bush
- **Weather notes** (late frost? extreme heat?)
- **First blossoms** and **harvest dates**
- **Fertilizing or pruning actions**
- **Any signs of pests or disease**
- **What worked (and what didn't)**

Tracking these things will help you:

- Notice patterns
- Adjust care based on real results
- Remember when and where you planted everything

Simple Tables to Use (Examples)

Tree /Plant	Planted	First Bloom	First Harvest	Notes
'Liberty' Apple	Mar 2025	April 2026	Sept 2027	Strong growth

Date	Action Taken	Weather	Observations
Apr 14	Pruned berry bushes	Rainy	Buds just forming

You can create your own journal using:

- A notebook
- A printable sheet
- A basic spreadsheet or app

Beginner tip: Review your notes at the start of each season to plan better!

Year-by-Year Improvement. Orchards are long-term projects.

With a diary, you'll grow your knowledge just like your trees—slowly, steadily, season by season.

Over time, your notes will become one of your most valuable tools. They'll help you plant smarter, prune better, and harvest more—year after year.

You're Not Just Planting Trees. You're Building a Legacy.

You've now learned the core foundations of a successful orchard: from choosing the right varieties, preparing your soil, planting with care, managing water, encouraging pollinators, and avoiding beginner mistakes.

But this is just the beginning.

In the next parts of this book, we'll dive deep into your specific USDA zone, so you can **fine-tune everything you've learned** to match your exact climate and conditions.

Whether you live in the frosty winters of Zone 6, the balanced seasons of Zone 7, or the long, warm days of Zone 8,

you're about to discover how to turn all of this knowledge into *results*—in your own backyard.

So take a deep breath, grab your notes, and get ready.

Your trees are waiting—and so is the harvest of a lifetime.

Chapter 2

GROWING IN USDA ZONE 6

Your Guide to Thriving in a Cold-Climate Orchard

 aybe your winters bite a little harder, your spring frosts hang on longer than expected, and your growing season feels just a bit too short.

But here's the truth: **Zone 6 is one of the most rewarding climates for fruit growers**—if you know how to work with it.

This section is written just for you.

It's where we zoom in on the **real-world challenges and smart strategies** that matter in your backyard—not someone else's.

You'll learn:

- Which **fruit trees and berries** thrive in your climate without drama
- How to **protect your plants from late frosts and sudden cold snaps**

- What **soil and water routines** work best in your zone
- How to time your planting, pruning, and harvesting to **maximize results in a short season**

You'll also discover how to build **a resilient orchard ecosystem** that handles winter stress naturally—no heavy chemicals, no guesswork.

Whether you're planting your first apple tree or expanding a full backyard food forest, this chapter gives you everything you need to grow strong, smart, and sustainable in Zone 6.

So grab your gloves and let's dig in.

Your cold-climate orchard journey starts right here.

Climate: Challenges and Opportunities

Zone 6 growers live in one of the most **climatically dynamic regions** of the country.

You get four true seasons, crisp autumns, and enough chill hours to grow some of the **best-tasting apples, pears, cherries, and hardy berries** in North America.

But it's not all smooth sailing.

Zone 6 comes with a few very specific challenges that we'll help you tackle—without repeating what you've already learned in Part 1.

The Challenges of Zone 6

1. Unpredictable Spring Frosts

Just when your trees start to bloom—bam!—a surprise cold snap hits. Late frosts are the #1 reason fruit sets fail in this zone.

What to do:

In this section, you'll learn **simple protection methods** (like row covers, microclimate tweaks, and late-blooming varieties) that make a huge difference.

2. Shorter Growing Season

In Zone 6, the frost-free window typically runs from **early May to mid-October**—which means you have about **150–170 days** to get everything done.

What to do:

We'll help you **choose early and mid-season varieties**, stagger your harvests, and plan care routines that match the rhythm of your climate—not the calendar.

3. Cold Winters and Soil Freezes

Winters in Zone 6 regularly dip to **–10°F to 0°F (–23°C to –18°C)**.

That's enough to **damage roots, crack bark**, or kill less-hardy species.

What to do:

We'll show you how to **choose naturally cold-resistant trees**, use mulch to insulate roots, and spot problem areas in your yard before you plant.

The Opportunities in Zone 6

Despite the cold, Zone 6 is rich with possibility.

> ➤ You get enough winter chill hours to grow **crisp, complex fruits** like apples, pears, and plums that struggle in warmer zones

> ➤ You can grow **hardy berries** that love cool nights: raspberries, blueberries, gooseberries, blackcurrants

> ➤ Your orchard has **natural pest suppression** in winter—fewer insects survive, which means less disease pressure

> ➤ You can use the changing seasons to **reset soil, rotate crops, and build long-term soil health**

In short: Zone 6 may make you wait longer for spring,

but when it arrives—it **rewards your patience** with flavor, freshness, and fruit that store beautifully.

What You'll Learn in This Section

Everything that follows in this part of the book is built to help Zone 6 growers:

- Choose trees and berries that **don't just survive, but thrive**
- Protect young plants from the cold **without needing expensive gear**
- Make the most of the shorter season with **zone-smart planning**
- Build a natural, productive orchard that comes back stronger each year

We'll build on what you learned in Part 1—and turn it into a plan **perfectly matched** to your local conditions.

Best Fruit Trees and Berries for Cold Climates

What to Grow for Strong Harvests in a Shorter Season

In Zone 6, your orchard needs to be tough—just like your winters. But here's the great news: this zone gives you access to **some of the most flavorful and cold-hardy fruit on the planet.**

Thanks to your solid winter chill and warm summer days, you can grow varieties that are:

- Packed with flavor
- Naturally disease-resistant
- Perfectly timed for your growing window

Here are the top-performing trees and berries

Apples (Malus domestica)

Cold-hardy apples are a **Zone 6 classic.** You'll get crisp, flavorful fruit and reliable yields.

Recommended varieties:

- **Liberty** – disease-resistant, sweet-tart, ripens mid-season
- **Enterprise** – long-keeping, great for storage, late harvest
- **Honeycrisp** – juicy, firm, excellent fresh-eating
- **Redfree** – early variety, resistant to scab and fire blight

Tip: Plant at least two different varieties for good cross-pollination.

Pears (Pyrus communis)

Many pears handle Zone 6 winters well, especially European types.

Recommended varieties:

- **Moonglow** – soft, juicy, and highly resistant to disease
- **Bartlett** – classic flavor, productive and cold-tolerant
- **Kieffer** – very hardy, great for canning and preserving

Tip: Pears ripen off the tree—harvest when firm, then let them soften indoors.

Cherries (Prunus spp.)

Choose cold-hardy sour and tart cherry types for best success.

Recommended varieties:

- **Montmorency** – the gold standard for pies, sauces, and freezing
- **North Star** – dwarf size, cold-hardy, self-pollinating
- **Meteor** – late bloomer, good for frost-prone areas

Tip: Cherries prefer well-drained soil and benefit from early spring pruning.

Peaches (Prunus persica)

Yes, you can grow peaches in Zone 6—**if you choose the right ones**.

Recommended varieties:

- **Reliance** – one of the hardiest peaches available
- **Contender** – sweet and juicy, good cold resistance
- **Madison** – reliable fruiting, even in cold springs

Tip: Peaches bloom early, so choose **late-blooming** varieties when possible to avoid frost damage.

Best Cold-Hardy Berries

Berries love Zone 6! You'll get **plenty of chill for strong flowering** and fruiting, especially if you plant in full sun.

Raspberries

- **Heritage** – everbearing, sweet and reliable
- **Latham** – classic red summer raspberry
- **Boyne** – very hardy, early season

Blueberries (Highbush types)

- **Patriot** – early, large berries, cold-hardy
- **Northblue** – compact, excellent for small spaces
- **Bluecrop** – mid-season, reliable producer

Tip: Blueberries need acidic soil (pH 4.5–5.5). Add pine mulch or peat moss to help.

Blackberries

- **Doyle** – thornless, high-yield, semi-hardy
- **Chester** – cold-hardy and resistant to cane diseases

Other Cold-Tolerant Fruits Worth Trying

- **Plums** – try 'Alderman' or 'Mount Royal' for reliability
- **Gooseberries** – super cold-hardy, easy to grow
- **Currants (red or black)** – tolerate cold and shade, great for jam or juicing
- **Elderberries** – thrive in wet spots, native to many northern areas

Quick Checklist:

- Cold-hardy (survive to –10°F / –23°C)
- Late bloomers (less risk of spring frost damage)
- Short-to-mid season harvest
- Disease resistance (especially scab, blight, and mildew)

With the right mix of trees and berries, your Zone 6 orchard will be **as resilient** as it is abundant—ready to deliver baskets of fruit with fewer worries about frost, pests, or stress.

In the next section, we'll focus on **how to protect your orchard from harsh winters and unpredictable spring frosts**, using low-cost, beginner-friendly techniques.

Winter and Frost Protection

Simple Strategies to Shield Your Orchard from Cold-Climate Stress

In Zone 6, your trees aren't just growing—they're surviving.

Cold winters and unpredictable spring frosts are **the two biggest threats** to young orchards in this region.

But with a few easy techniques, you can help your plants **get through the cold and come back stronger each year.**

How to Protect Fruit Trees in Winter

During winter, the biggest risks are:

- **Root damage** from deep soil freezes
- **Bark cracking** (aka "frost splitting") from sudden temperature swings
- **Animal damage** from hungry deer, rabbits, or rodents

Easy Winter Protection Tips:

1. Apply Thick Mulch Before the First Frost

- Use 4–6 inches (10–15 cm) of mulch around the base of trees
- Helps insulate roots and regulate soil temperature
- Use straw, wood chips, shredded leaves—**not compost**

Keep mulch **2–4 inches away from the trunk** to prevent rot.

2. Wrap Young Tree Trunks

- ➤ Use tree wrap or plastic spiral guards
- Prevents sunscald and bark cracking in freezing temps

- Also discourages mice and rabbits from chewing bark

Wrap in late fall and remove in early spring.

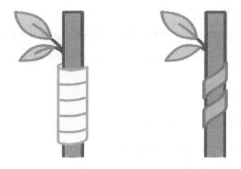

3. Protect Against Browsing Animals

- ➢ Use wire cages or fencing around young trees
- Deer and rabbits often target bark and twigs when food is scarce
- Commercial animal repellents (natural sprays) can help too

4. Avoid Late-Season Fertilizing

- Fertilizing too close to frost encourages soft new growth
- Stop feeding trees **by late summer** so they harden off before winter

Spring Frosts: Protect Blossoms, Save Fruit

Spring frosts in Zone 6 often arrive **after trees have started to bloom**, which can kill flowers and destroy that year's fruit before it even forms.

Frost Protection Methods (Simple but Powerful):

1. Choose Late-Blooming Varieties

- One of the best long-term strategies
- Late bloomers are less likely to be hit by frost
- Apples, plums, and pears have excellent late-blooming options (see previous section)

2. Use Row Covers or Frost Blankets

- On cold nights (below 32°F / 0°C), cover small trees or bushes
- Use frost cloth, old sheets, or floating row cover
- Drape all the way to the ground to trap warmth

Remove during the day to avoid overheating.

3. Water the Soil Before a Frost

- Moist soil holds heat better than dry soil
- Water in the afternoon before a frost is expected to **help retain ground warmth**

4. Use Windbreaks and Thermal Mass

- Plant hedges or place barriers to block cold wind
- Large stones, barrels of water, or dark-colored mulch can absorb heat during the day and release it at night

Quick Checklist:

- Mulch deeply in fall to insulate roots
- Wrap trunks of young trees
- Fence off trees to prevent animal damage
- Stop fertilizing in late summer
- Cover trees during spring frost events
- Water soil before frost to trap ground heat
- Choose late-blooming varieties to avoid blossom loss

With just a little preparation, your Zone 6 orchard can handle cold nights and frosty mornings like a pro.

And the reward?

A healthy, fruit-filled growing season ahead.

In the next section, we'll talk about how to **optimize irrigation and seasonal care** in Zone 6—so your trees grow strong from spring to fall, without wasting time or water.

Annual Irrigation and Care Program

Growing fruit trees in Zone 6 means working with the rhythm of nature. From frozen winters to warm, fast-moving summers, each season asks for something different.

Here's a **season-by-season guide** to help you keep your orchard healthy, hydrated, and on track—without overcomplicating your routine.

Spring (March–May)

Focus: Wake-up, protect blossoms, encourage growth

Tasks:

- Remove winter wraps and inspect trunks for damage
- Clean up fallen branches and winter mulch if needed
- Apply fresh mulch (2–4 inches) around trees and berries
- Prune stone fruits (like peaches and cherries) before buds open
- Monitor for early pests (like aphids)

Watering:

- Begin watering when the soil starts to dry out
- Water deeply **once or twice a week**, depending on rainfall
- Avoid overhead watering on cool days to reduce disease risk

Tip: Avoid heavy spraying during bloom—protect your pollinators!

Summer (June–August)

Focus: Water, protect, and manage rapid growth

Tasks:

- Monitor trees weekly for signs of pests, drought stress, or fungal issues
- Remove suckers and water sprouts as needed
- Prune lightly to improve airflow (especially for dense berries)
- Fertilize only if needed—don't overfeed

Watering:

- Deep water young trees and berries **1–2x per week**
- Use drip irrigation or soaker hoses to avoid leaf diseases
- Increase watering during heat waves
- Mulch helps retain moisture and reduce watering needs

Tip: Water in early morning or late afternoon to reduce evaporation.

Fall (September–November)

Focus: Prepare for dormancy and build resilience

Tasks:

- Harvest remaining fruit and remove any fallen or rotting fruit
- Prune only if absolutely necessary (avoid major cuts)
- Stop fertilizing by early fall
- Apply a final layer of mulch around the base of trees
- Clean and store tools for winter
- Inspect for diseases or pests and remove infected material

Watering:

- Keep watering **until the ground begins to freeze**, especially after dry autumns
- Water deeply once every 10–14 days if rainfall is low

Tip: Late watering helps trees store moisture before winter dormancy.

Winter (December–February)

Focus: Protection and observation

Tasks:

- Wrap young tree trunks to prevent sunscald and rodent damage
- Check mulch coverage and replenish if needed
- Avoid pruning in deep cold—wait until late winter
- Review your orchard diary and plan for spring

Watering:

- No regular watering is needed unless there's an extended dry spell (uncommon in Zone 6)

Tip: This is a great time to research new varieties or order bare-root trees for spring!

Quick Overview Table

Season	Focus	Watering	Key Actions
Spring	Growth & protection	Deep water 1–2x/week	Prune, mulch, protect blossoms
Summer	Hydration & health	Deep water regularly	Monitor pests, light pruning, fertilize
Fall	Transition & cleanup	Water until freeze	Harvest, mulch, stop feeding
Winter	Protection & planning	Minimal (if dry only)	Wrap trunks, plan, review diary

Stick to this seasonal rhythm and **adjust based on your microclimate**. No two years are the same—but with good notes and observation, you'll spot patterns and respond better each season.

In the next section, we'll explore how to use **permaculture in Zone 6** to build resilience into your orchard—so it can thrive with less input and more natural support.

Permaculture for Cold Climates

When you think of permaculture, you might imagine warm, tropical gardens overflowing with bananas and exotic plants.

But the truth is, **permaculture works just as well—and maybe even better—in cold climates like Zone 6.**

Why?

Because when your growing season is short and your winters are tough, nature-based strategies help you do **more with less.**

Let's look at how to apply permaculture principles in a way that makes sense for Zone 6.

1. Use the Landscape to Your Advantage

In Zone 6, winter winds, snow buildup, and cold air pockets are real challenges. Instead of fighting them, design **with them.**

Simple strategies:

- **Plant windbreaks** (like hazelnuts, elderberries, or evergreens) on the north and west sides of your orchard
- Use **slopes and natural dips** to place cold-hardy species where air settles
- Place **less hardy trees** on higher ground or south-facing slopes for warmth
- Add **thermal mass** (stones, barrels, compost piles) near sensitive trees to store and release heat

Tip: Observe how snow melts in your yard—it shows you where warmth and cold linger.

2. Build Soil the Permaculture Way

In cold zones, building and protecting your soil is key.

Cold slows microbial activity—so the more life you add, the faster your soil improves.

Cold-climate techniques:

- **Deep mulching**: use leaves, straw, and wood chips to insulate and feed the soil
- **Lasagna gardening**: layer compost, cardboard, grass clippings in fall so they break down by spring
- **Comfrey, clover, and dandelions**: cold-hardy "dynamic accumulators" that improve soil without tilling

3. Stack Functions with Cold-Hardy Companions

Permaculture loves plants that "do more than one thing."

In Zone 6, choose **cold-hardy companions** that help your trees thrive.

Example Guild for Zone 6 Apple Tree:

- **Comfrey**: nutrient mining + mulch material
- **Chives**: repel pests + edible
- **Yarrow**: attracts pollinators + improves soil
- **White clover**: ground cover + nitrogen fixer
- **Calendula**: attracts beneficial insects + self-seeds yearly

These plants all survive winter and bounce back strong in spring.

4. Harvest and Store Water Naturally

Water can be unpredictable in Zone 6—wet springs, dry summers, and frozen winters.

Easy permaculture water tricks:

- **Swales**: shallow trenches on slopes that capture spring rain and snowmelt
- **Rain barrels**: collect water in spring to use during dry midsummer weeks
- **Mulch basins**: build shallow bowls around trees and fill with mulch to hold moisture

These methods store water **in the soil**, where your trees need it most.

5. Think Long-Term, Build Slowly

Permaculture is about **building systems that improve over time**—not instant results.

Start simple:

- One guild around one tree
- One rain barrel
- One new native hedge

Add more each season as you learn what works in your space.

Quick Recap:

- Use natural windbreaks and slopes for shelter
- Build deep, living soil with mulch and compost
- Plant multi-purpose cold-hardy companions
- Catch and store water with swales, barrels, and mulch
- Grow slow, observe, and improve every year

Permaculture in Zone 6 isn't about perfection—it's about **creating a system that works with your climate**, builds resilience, and gives you more food with less input over time.

In the next section, we'll pull it all together into a **month-by-month calendar** for your Zone 6 orchard—so you know exactly what to do and when.

Annual Orchard Care Calendar

In Zone 6, success comes from **timing** as much as technique.

With cold winters, late frosts, and a shorter growing season, you need to act at the right moment—not too early, not too late.

Here's your **month-by-month guide** to caring for your fruit trees and berries in Zone 6.

Use it as a checklist each year to stay on track and in sync with nature.

Late Winter / Early Spring (February–March)

- Prune apple, pear, and stone fruit trees before buds break
- Check for rodent damage and remove trunk wraps
- Clean tools and sharpen pruning shears
- Apply dormant oil spray (if using) to prevent pests
- Order or pick up bare-root trees and berry plants

Mid to Late Spring (April–May)

- Plant new trees and berries once soil is workable
- Mulch around trees (2–4 inches, away from the trunk)
- Start watering regularly if rainfall is low
- Watch for aphids, caterpillars, or fungal leaf spots
- Thin fruit on overloaded branches after blossom drop
- Protect blossoms from frost using row covers if needed

Early Summer (June)

- Deep water young trees and bushes 1–2 times per week
- Prune out water sprouts and suckers
- Net berries to protect from birds
- Fertilize if needed with compost or slow-release organic feed
- Monitor for signs of stress, yellowing leaves, or pests

Mid to Late Summer (July–August)

- Harvest early berries and fruit (raspberries, cherries, early apples)
- Keep watering during dry periods
- Refresh mulch if it's breaking down
- Light summer pruning for airflow (especially on overgrown bushes)
- Stop fertilizing by mid-August to avoid soft late growth

Early Fall (September)

- Harvest apples, pears, plums, and fall berries
- Remove fallen fruit and debris to prevent pests
- Light cleanup pruning only (avoid major cuts)
- Collect seeds, take notes in your orchard diary
- Start planning for next season

Late Fall (October–November)

- Rake up leaves and compost disease-free material
- Apply a fresh layer of mulch before the first frost
- Wrap young trunks to protect against frost cracks and rodents
- Water deeply before ground freezes if rainfall is low
- Install tree guards or fencing if deer and rabbits are active

Winter (December–January)

- Rest and observe—no pruning or fertilizing
- Review your orchard journal: what worked, what didn't
- Dream, sketch, and plan for spring
- Order new trees or varieties
- Attend local workshops or read up on Zone 6 fruit-growing tips

Summary Table – Zone 6 Monthly Orchard Care

Month	Key Tasks
Feb–Mar	Prune trees, prep tools, check for damage
Apr–May	Planting, mulching, pest watch, blossom protection
June	Watering, netting berries, early harvesting
July–Aug	Peak harvesting, summer pruning, stop fertilizing
Sept	Fall harvest, cleanup, notes
Oct–Nov	Mulch, wrap trees, deep water before frost
Dec–Jan	Rest, review, plan, order new plants

Patience, observation, and smart timing will take you further than perfection ever could.

In Zone 6, success doesn't come from doing everything "by the book." It comes from learning to read *your* land—the way the snow melts, the way the wind moves through your orchard, the way your trees respond to each season.

Use this calendar as a compass, not a cage. There will be years when spring comes late, or a sudden frost surprises even the most experienced growers. That's not failure—it's nature being nature.

What matters is that you **show up consistently**, observe closely, and make small, smart decisions every season.

Because fruit growing isn't about control. It's about building **a relationship** with your climate, your soil, your trees—and yourself.

Some years will bring baskets of fruit. Others will bring lessons. Both are valuable. Both help you grow.

So trust the process, enjoy the journey, and remember:

A great orchard is built one season at a time—and you're already doing the most important thing: starting.

Now, if you live in USDA Zone 7, get ready—your growing window is a bit longer, and your opportunities even wider.

Chapter 3

GROWING IN USDA ZONE 7

Balanced Seasons, Bigger Possibilities

Welcome to USDA Zone 7—where fruit trees find a little more room to breathe. Your winters are milder, your springs arrive sooner, and your growing season stretches longer than in colder zones. But don't let that lull you into thinking less care is needed—because in Zone 7, **success depends on balance**.

This section is designed specifically for your climate. We'll focus on:

- Choosing varieties that love the **extra warmth but still handle winter**
- Managing **early growth spurts** without risking frost damage
- Adapting watering, pruning, and harvest timing to fit your **longer season**
- Using nature-based strategies to keep your orchard **resilient, efficient, and productive**

You've got more options here—but that also means more choices to get right. Let's make sure you plant smart, care wisely, and **take full advantage of everything Zone 7 offers**. Ready to grow with confidence? Let's get started.

Zone 7 Climate:

If you garden in USDA Zone 7, you're in one of the most forgiving—and promising—regions for growing fruit trees and berries.

This zone offers a **rare balance**: winters that are cold enough for many fruit trees to thrive, and summers that are warm enough to ensure full ripening.

That balance opens the door to a **greater variety of fruits**, a longer growing season, and a lower risk of frost damage compared to colder zones.

Let's explore what makes Zone 7 special—and how to use it to your advantage.

A Longer Growing Season = More Options

Your **frost-free period** typically runs from **early April to late October**. That gives you around **200–220 growing days** per year.

What that means for you:

- More time for trees to mature, flower, and fruit
- Greater flexibility for planting, pruning, and harvesting
- The ability to grow both **cold-hardy** and **moderate-climate varieties**

You can enjoy everything from classic apples and pears to figs, persimmons, and even some cold-tolerant citrus in sheltered spots.

Milder Winters, Fewer Surprises

Your winters are cool, but not brutal.

Typical low temperatures stay between **0°F and 10°F (–18°C to –12°C)**, which provides just enough chill hours for most temperate fruit trees, **without risking severe freeze damage**.

This means:

- Less winter stress on young trees
- Greater survival rates for marginal or borderline-hardy varieties

- Fewer worries about root damage or trunk cracking

You still need to **monitor for sudden temperature drops**, especially in early spring, but the overall winter conditions are much easier to manage than in Zones 6 or 5.

Early Springs = Earlier Growth (and Earlier Risks)

Spring arrives sooner in Zone 7—but that doesn't mean it's always smooth sailing.

Warm spells can wake up your trees early… only for a **late frost to damage tender buds**.

To manage this:

- Focus on late-blooming varieties if possible
- Avoid heavy pruning in late winter, which can stimulate early growth
- Keep row covers or frost blankets handy just in case
- Choose planting sites with good air drainage (frost settles in low spots)

This small risk is manageable—and the reward is earlier harvests and longer production windows.

Warm Summers = Rich Flavor and Bigger Yields

Summer in Zone 7 is typically **long, sunny, and stable**, with fewer extreme heat spikes than southern zones.

This gives your trees the time they need to:

- Fully ripen fruit
- Build sugar and flavor
- Develop strong roots and sturdy branches
- With proper watering and mulch, you can grow robust crops of **peaches, nectarines, berries, plums, apples**, and more—with fewer fungal issues than in humid southern zones.

Zone 7 gives you:

- **More flexibility** in what you can plant
- **Less weather-related stress** than colder zones
- **A longer harvest season** with better fruit quality
- The opportunity to grow both **northern favorites and southern newcomers**

It's the perfect zone for experimenting, expanding, and enjoying a **diverse, productive home orchard**.

In the next section, we'll explore the best trees and berries for Zone 7—so you can build a fruit garden that thrives from early spring to late fall.

Let's make the most of your growing zone.

Best Fruit Trees and Berries for Long Seasons

With around **220 frost-free days per year**, Zone 7 gives you a powerful advantage: **time**.

Time to plant. Time to grow. And most importantly—**time to harvest again and again**.

By selecting the right mix of fruit trees and berries, you can plan a season that starts in **early June** and stretches into **late October**.

Here's how to build your orchard for **continuous, overlapping harvests** using cold-tolerant and heat-friendly varieties.

Start with Stone Fruits – Early to Mid-Summer Delights

Zone 7 is ideal for growing peaches, plums, nectarines, and apricots—fruits that need a bit more heat than northern zones can offer.

Recommended Varieties:

- **Peaches:**
    - *Redhaven* – mid-July, juicy and reliable
    - *Contender* – late July, cold-tolerant, rich flavor
    - *Elberta* – late August, classic flavor, large fruit
- **Plums:**
    - *Methley* – early ripening, self-fertile
    - *Ozark Premier* – sweet, large red plums, late summer
- **Nectarines:**
    - *Fantasia* – late ripening, intense flavor
- **Apricots:**
    - *Goldcot* – cold-hardy, good for fresh eating or drying
    - *Moorpark* – excellent flavor, ripens mid to late summer

Tip: Protect early bloomers from spring frost by planting in slightly elevated or protected spots.

Apples and Pears – From Late Summer into Fall

Zone 7 lets you grow both **early and late varieties**, so you can extend the apple and pear harvest into October.

Apples:

- *Gala* – early harvest, crisp and sweet
- *Liberty* – disease-resistant, ripens late August
- *Enterprise* – late season, excellent storage
- *Fuji* – late October, best flavor when grown with full sun

Pears:

- *Bartlett* – juicy, mid-season
- *Shenandoah* – fire blight resistant, ripens late
- *Magness* – soft, sweet, harvests in early fall

Tip: Combine early and late varieties for a harvest that spans 6–8 weeks.

Berries for the Full Season

Berries love Zone 7's balanced sun and soil conditions.

With smart variety selection, you can harvest **from late May to early October.**

Blueberries (Highbush types):

- *Duke* – early season
- *Bluecrop* – mid-season
- *Elliott* – late season

Raspberries:

- *Caroline* – everbearing, from June to frost
- *Heritage* – long season, high yield
- *Fallgold* – yellow fruit, sweet and productive

Blackberries:

- *Natchez* – early, thornless
- *Triple Crown* – mid-late, high yield
- *Prime-Ark Freedom* – everbearing, fruits on first-year canes

Tip: Prune berry bushes in late winter and mulch well to preserve moisture during the warm months.

Bonus Crops for Extended Seasons

Zone 7 also opens the door to some **borderline warm-climate crops** that wouldn't survive in colder zones:

- **Figs** (*Celeste, Chicago Hardy*) – ripen in late summer, may produce a second crop
- **Persimmons** (*American or Asian types*) – harvest in October and even into November
- **Pawpaws** – tropical flavor, cold-hardy, ready in September
- **Pomegranates** (*Russian varieties*) – in protected microclimates only

These fruits are ideal for **sunny, south-facing walls or sheltered corners** of your garden.

Quick Planning Strategy: Stagger Your Harvests

To take full advantage of Zone 7's long season:

1. **Choose early, mid, and late-season varieties** for each fruit type
2. **Mix species** (peach + apple + fig + raspberry) for variety and reliability
3. **Plan for succession**: when one fruit finishes, another begins
4. **Add everbearing berries** for continuous picking

Zone 7 offers you a rare opportunity: to enjoy fresh fruit **over five full months**—with the right varieties and a little planning.

From the first berries in spring to the last apples and persimmons in fall, your orchard can become a **living calendar of flavor.**

In the next section, we'll explore how to protect your trees from **heat stress, pests, and unpredictable weather**—so your long season stays productive from start to finish.

Maximizing Growth and Fruit Production

With longer days, warmer nights, and a generous growing season, Zone 7 gives you everything you need to grow healthy, productive fruit trees and berry bushes.

But to really **unlock their full potential,** you need to help your plants **use that time wisely**.

This section will show you how to:

- Boost vegetative growth without overstimulating
- Time pruning and feeding for maximum fruit production
- Keep energy focused where it matters—**on quality fruit, not just green leaves**

Let's turn that long season into real results.

Support Strong, Balanced Vegetative Growth

The vegetative phase—when your plant is focused on growing leaves, stems, and roots—is the foundation for future fruiting.

In Zone 7, this phase can be **longer than in colder zones**, which means you need to **guide the growth**, not just let it run wild.

What to do:

- **Prune early in the season** to shape growth and direct energy
- **Use balanced organic fertilizers** (like compost tea or fish emulsion) early on—avoid high nitrogen past midsummer
- **Thin out dense growth** to allow sunlight and airflow into the canopy

Too much growth = more disease risk + less fruit. Keep your trees open, upright, and focused.

Encourage Flowering and Fruit Set

In Zone 7, it's easy for trees to put on leaves... but you want them to put out flowers and fruit, too.

Key strategies:

- Choose fruiting varieties with a reliable chill-hour match
- Avoid overfeeding—especially nitrogen, which delays flowering
- Mulch well in spring to retain moisture and reduce stress
- Water consistently during flowering and early fruit set (drought = blossom drop)

For berries, remove weak canes, and support the healthiest shoots with trellising or stakes for better air and sun exposure.

Smart Summer Pruning = More Fruit, Less Waste

Don't fear pruning during the season—Zone 7 included.

Summer pruning:

- Controls excessive leafy growth
- Redirects energy into ripening fruit

- Improves airflow (reducing mold, mildew, pests)

Focus on:

- Removing suckers and water sprouts
- Cutting back overgrown branches that block light
- Clearing low-hanging limbs that crowd the base

Do it **in the early morning or late afternoon** to avoid sunburn on exposed branches.

Optimize Watering to Prevent Stress

Too much water? You'll get soft fruit and fungal problems.

Too little? Fruit shrivels, drops early, or splits.

Best practice in Zone 7:

- Use **drip irrigation or soaker hoses** to deliver steady, deep moisture
- **Mulch heavily** to keep soil cool and prevent evaporation
- Water deeply **once or twice a week**—more during heatwaves

Bonus: Add comfrey or nettle tea (as a foliar spray or soil drench) once a month to feed plants naturally during high production.

Remove, Thin, and Redirect to Improve Quality

More fruit doesn't always mean better fruit.

In a long season, thinning fruits can dramatically improve:

- Size
- Flavor
- Resistance to splitting or cracking

For trees:

- Remove 1–2 small fruits from every cluster early in the season
- Aim for **one strong fruit per 6–8 inches of branch**

For berries:

- Harvest frequently to encourage new flowering

- Remove small or diseased fruits to reduce stress on the plant

Checklist

- Prune early for shape, prune lightly in summer for control
- Feed moderately—more in spring, less in summer
- Water deeply and regularly; mulch to hold moisture
- Thin fruit to boost size and sweetness
- Use airflow, sunlight, and spacing as tools for health

In Zone 7, your growing season gives you room to grow—but also space to waste.

With the right timing and attention, you can **shift the balance from "green growth" to "fruitful growth."**

You don't need to push your orchard—just **guide it.**

And as the weeks go by, your trees will thank you with more color, more flavor, and more harvest than you thought possible.

In the next section, we'll talk about how to **protect your orchard from late-season threats** like heat, pests, and overproduction—so you end strong, not stressed.

Moisture, Pest & Disease Control Naturally

Zone 7's warm summers and balanced rainfall are perfect for fruit development—but also ideal for **fungal diseases and pest outbreaks.** To keep your orchard productive, you'll need to **manage moisture wisely** and build a natural defense system that protects your plants **without constant spraying.**

Let's break it down step by step.

1. Manage Moisture Before It Becomes a Problem

Excess moisture = fungal growth, root rot, and fruit splitting.

The goal isn't to dry things out—it's to keep water **where it's needed** (in the roots), and **out of where it causes trouble** (on leaves and fruit).

How to manage moisture in Zone 7:

- **Use mulch** (2–4 inches) to keep soil moist and cool—but keep it away from the trunk to avoid rot
- **Avoid overhead watering**—use drip irrigation or soaker hoses instead
- **Water early in the morning** to give leaves time to dry
- **Prune for airflow**—especially in berry bushes and dense tree canopies
- **Remove dropped fruit or leaves** promptly—they're magnets for rot and fungus

2. Natural Protection Against Common Fungal Diseases

In Zone 7, the most common threats are:

- Powdery mildew
- Leaf spot
- Brown rot (especially on stone fruits)
- Fire blight (on pears and apples)

Natural sprays to prevent or slow disease:

- **Neem oil** – antifungal, safe for fruit and pollinators if sprayed early or late in the day
- **Baking soda + castile soap** – homemade spray to reduce mildew
- **Copper fungicide** – for organic use (apply with care, avoid overuse)
- **Garlic or horsetail tea** – strengthens plant resistance

Prevention is key: begin light applications **before symptoms appear**, especially during humid weeks.

3. Smart Strategies to Control Insects Naturally

Insects don't destroy healthy orchards overnight—but **unchecked populations** can reduce harvest and weaken trees.

Common pests in Zone 7:

Aphids (curling leaves, sticky residue)

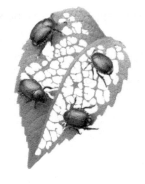

Japanese beetles (skeletonized leaves)

Spider mites (fine webs, yellow spots)

Codling moths (worms inside apples)

Fruit flies (on overripe or damaged fruit)

4. Organic control methods:

- **Introduce beneficial insects** (ladybugs, lacewings, parasitic wasps)
- **Use neem or insecticidal soap** as a first defense
- **Hang sticky traps** or pheromone traps for moths and flies
- **Spray kaolin clay** to deter beetles and sun damage on fruit
- **Plant companions** like garlic, marigold, nasturtium to repel invaders

Tip: Keep diverse flowers blooming near your orchard to attract predators of pests.

5. Resilience Through Observation & Prevention

Reactive spraying only goes so far.

True success comes from building an **ecosystem that naturally defends itself**—and from catching issues early.

Weekly "health check" routine:

- Walk your orchard in the morning
- Check the undersides of leaves
- Look for holes, spots, curls, or sticky residue
- Touch the soil—if it feels soggy or cracked, adjust your watering
- Take notes in your orchard diary to track what works and what doesn't

Quick Action Plan – Moisture & Pest Management in Zone 7

- Use drip irrigation to avoid wet leaves
- Mulch generously, but keep it off trunks

- Prune for air circulation and sunlight
- Spray natural antifungals during humid weeks
- Introduce and protect beneficial insects
- Use traps and companion planting to reduce pressure
- Observe weekly—respond early, act small

In Zone 7, moisture is both your best friend and your biggest risk. The key to long-term success is **balance**: keep the roots hydrated, the leaves dry, and the environment inviting for allies—not invaders.

Your job isn't to fight nature—it's to listen to it, guide it, and respond with smart, simple actions.

In the next section, we'll prepare for the final stretch of the season—**how to finish strong with fall care, proper harvest timing, and preparing your orchard for winter.**

Applying Permaculture in Mixed Climates

Zone 7 is what we call a **"mixed climate"**:

- Winters are cold—but not extreme
- Summers are warm—but not tropical
- Rainfall is seasonal—but not always reliable

This means you face **variety**, not extremes. And that's great news for permaculture—because mixed climates respond beautifully to **smart, layered, nature-based design.**

Let's look at how to build a fruit tree system that **thrives in diversity**, stays healthy with less effort, and **works with the land**, not against it.

1. Observe First, Then Design

In permaculture, everything starts with **observation.**

Before planting or changing anything, take time to notice:

- Where the sun hits in different seasons

- Where water flows or pools
- Where wind and shade naturally occur
- Which spots dry out faster (or stay soggy longer)

Then design accordingly:

- Dry, sunny zones = drought-tolerant herbs, figs, grapes
- Moist zones = currants, elderberries, gooseberries
- Cold pockets = late-blooming apples, plums, or nitrogen-fixing shrubs

This isn't guesswork—it's **design that fits your yard**, not someone else's diagram.

2. Fruit Tree Guilds for Mixed Conditions

A **fruit tree guild** is a group of plants that support a central fruit tree by offering nutrients, pest protection, moisture control, and biodiversity.

In Zone 7, your guilds must be **adaptive**—able to handle both rain and drought, both sun and shade.

Example: Zone 7 Peach Tree Guild

- **Main Tree**: Peach (requires airflow and drainage)
- **Companions**:
    o *Yarrow* – attracts beneficial insects
    o *Comfrey* – dynamic accumulator + chop-and-drop mulch
    o *Garlic or chives* – repel borers and aphids
    o *White clover* – nitrogen fixer + ground cover
    o *Thyme or oregano* – hardy ground cover that handles both heat and drought

These plants survive variable conditions and reduce your workload.

3.Water Harvesting with Smart Drainage

In mixed climates, water is a game of **"just enough, but not too much."**

Here's how to design your orchard to hold moisture when it matters—and shed it when it doesn't:

- Create **swales** (shallow ditches) on contour to catch spring rains
- Add **mulch basins** under trees to store water around the roots
- Use **rain barrels** from rooftops to irrigate during dry weeks
- Elevate trees on mounds in soggy zones to protect roots
- Direct excess water into **overflow basins** with fruiting shrubs

Good water design = fewer disease problems + less summer stress.

4. Encourage Biodiversity (and Let It Work for You)

Biodiversity isn't just nice to have—it's your natural defense system.

In Zone 7, include:

- Pollinator strips with **lavender, echinacea, mint, bee balm**
- Native shrubs for wildlife and beneficial insects (elderberry, viburnum)
- Companion plants that repel pests (marigold, tansy, nasturtium)
- A variety of fruiting times to keep beneficial insects active longer

This reduces your need for spraying, fertilizing, and constant intervention.

5. Think Layers, Not Rows

Permaculture favors **layered design**, not neat rows.

Use vertical space and seasonal cycles to get more from less.

In Zone 7, you can plant:

- **Overstory**: fruit trees (apple, pear, peach)
- **Understory**: berry bushes (currants, raspberries)
- **Ground cover**: herbs (thyme, oregano), clover
- **Root layer**: garlic, onions
- **Vertical layer**: trellised beans or grapes
- **Fungal layer**: wine cap mushrooms in shaded mulch

This mimics a forest edge—resilient, diverse, productive.

Quick Recap :

Observe sun, water, wind, and soil before planting

- Choose fruit tree guilds that tolerate shifting conditions
- Catch and store water with swales and mulch basins
- Encourage biodiversity to reduce pests and improve resilience
- Design in layers, not rows, for higher yield with lower input

In a mixed climate, **flexibility is strength**.

The weather may shift—but if your orchard is rooted in observation, biodiversity, and smart layering, it will **adapt and thrive** without constant correction.

Permaculture in Zone 7 isn't just possible—it's powerful.

Let nature carry part of the load, and you'll find that your orchard becomes more productive, more beautiful, and more sustainable with every passing year.

Next, we'll turn everything you've learned into a **monthly action plan**, with a detailed **care calendar for Zone 7**.

Annual Orchard Care Calendar

Late Winter / Early Spring (February–March)

Wake up the orchard, prep your soil, protect early buds.

Tasks:

- Prune apples, pears, and stone fruits before bud break
- Clean up winter mulch, branches, and debris
- Apply dormant oil spray if needed
- Finish planting bare-root trees
- Begin composting and soil enrichment
- Start seeds for guild companions or pollinator plants indoors

Watering: Start watering newly planted trees if the soil dries out.

Mid to Late Spring (April–May)

Plant, mulch, and watch for rapid growth—and pests.

Tasks:

- Plant new trees and shrubs
- Add mulch (2–4 inches) around trees and berries
- Monitor for aphids, caterpillars, fungal signs
- Apply first foliar feed (compost tea, seaweed, etc.)
- Stake or trellis berry canes
- Thin fruit after blossom drop for size and quality
- Begin regular orchard journaling

Watering: Water deeply once or twice a week, depending on rainfall.

Early Summer (June)

Manage moisture, airflow, and direct energy into fruit production.

Tasks:

- Prune water sprouts and low suckers
- Harvest early berries
- Fertilize lightly if growth is weak

- Use neem oil or organic soap sprays preventively
- Net trees and bushes against birds
- Observe pollination success and set

Watering: Keep moisture consistent—especially for young trees and fruit set.

Mid to Late Summer (July–August)

Focus on hydration, heat stress, pest management, and light pruning.

Tasks:

- Deep mulch to preserve moisture
- Monitor for fruit flies, beetles, and mildew
- Light pruning for airflow
- Stop fertilizing by mid-August
- Continue harvesting berries, peaches, plums
- Take notes on which varieties are thriving

Watering: Deep watering 1–2x/week depending on heat and soil.

Early Fall (September)

Harvest season ramps up—prepare for transition.

Tasks:

- Harvest apples, pears, figs, and late berries
- Remove any fallen or diseased fruit
- Light pruning only if needed
- Sow cover crops or ground cover under trees
- Begin fall composting with leaves and garden waste

Watering: Reduce watering gradually unless the weather is hot and dry.

Late Fall (October–November)

Protect roots, finish cleanup, and prepare for dormancy.

Tasks:

- Final harvests (persimmons, late apples)

- Apply thick winter mulch (5–6 inches) around tree bases
- Wrap young trunks (tree guards or spirals)
- Remove nets, tools, irrigation components
- Review your orchard diary and adjust plans for next year

Watering: Deep water before the ground freezes if the fall is dry.

Winter (December–January)

Rest, observe, plan, and prepare.

Tasks:

- Review your orchard notes and adjust your planting map
- Order new trees and seeds
- Attend a local workshop or read a book to deepen your knowledge
- Repair tools and sharpen pruners
- Walk the orchard during warm spells to check for damage

Watering: Not usually needed, unless there's a dry, mild spell.

Summary Table –Monthly Orchard Care

Month	Focus	Actions
Feb–Mar	Pruning and prep	Clean, prune, plant bare root, spray dormant oil
Apr–May	Planting and protection	Mulch, pest check, foliar feed, thin fruit
June	Growth and training	Prune light, fertilize, manage insects
July–Aug	Heat and hydration	Deep water, mulch, pest control, harvest
Sept	Harvest and observe	Pick fruit, sow cover crops, compost, journaling
Oct–Nov	Protection and winter	Final mulch, wrap trunks, clean up,

	prep	reflect
Dec–Jan	Rest and learning	Review notes, plan, order trees, sharpen tools

This calendar is your **guiding rhythm**, not a rigid schedule.

Each year is a little different—but your trees will teach you what works, as long as you're paying attention.

Zone 7 gives you a **long, generous window to work with**.

So take advantage of it by planning with the seasons—not against them—and letting your orchard evolve one layer, one branch, one harvest at a time.

In the next section, we'll dive into USDA **Zone 8**, where the heat intensifies and fruit possibilities expand even further.

But for now, if you live in Zone 7—you're already in one of the best climates for fruit-growing success.

Chapter 4

GROWING IN USDA ZONE 8

Welcome to Zone 8—where the sun stays longer, the soil warms earlier, and the fruit possibilities expand beyond what northern growers could dream of.

If you live in this zone, you're in one of the most **fruit-friendly climates in the country**. Your growing season can stretch beyond **8 months**, and your winters are mild enough to support a wide range of **both traditional and exotic fruits**.

But with more opportunity comes new challenges:

- **Heat stress** in mid-summer
- **Pest pressure** that lasts longer
- **Water management** in dry spells
- And the need to **choose the right varieties** that can handle the warmth *without losing flavor or structure*

In this part of the book, you'll discover:

- Which fruit trees and berries thrive in Zone 8's unique conditions
- How to manage irrigation, heat, and overgrowth effectively
- How to use permaculture to protect your orchard and boost yields naturally
- And how to create a harvest calendar that **starts early and ends late**

Whether you dream of growing peaches, figs, citrus, or year-round berries, this is the chapter that helps you **turn long seasons into lasting abundance**.

Let's dive in—Zone 8 is ready to produce.

Zone 8 Climate

Living in USDA Zone 8 means you have one of the longest and most generous growing seasons in the country.

With **200 to 240 frost-free days per year**, you can grow **earlier, longer, and more** than gardeners in colder climates.

But that luxury comes with its own rules.

To make the most of Zone 8's climate, you need to:

- Embrace the heat—but manage it
- Use the early spring start wisely
- Stretch your harvests without stressing your plants
- Protect your orchard from overexposure, drought, and pests that love the warmth as much as your fruit does

Let's explore what makes this climate special—and how to work with it instead of against it.

An Early Start = Early Growth (and Early Responsibility)

Spring in Zone 8 starts fast.

Trees begin to leaf out in **February or March**, and some early-blooming varieties may flower by the end of winter.

What this means for you:

- You can plant earlier—but you must be ready
- **Late frosts are still possible**—especially in shaded or low-lying areas
- Early pests (like aphids and borers) can appear sooner than expected
- Pruning and feeding should happen **before growth explodes**, not after

Solution: Use **microclimate observation** to plant early but smart—choose higher ground, good air flow, and sun-trapping spots.

Hot Summers: Energy, Growth... and Stress

By mid-summer, Zone 8 temperatures often hover between **85–100°F (29–38°C)**, with strong sun and occasional droughts.

While fruit trees love the heat for ripening sugars and building flavor, too much can:

- Cause **sunburn on fruits and branches**
- Trigger **fruit drop** if watering is inconsistent
- Invite a wide range of **insects, mites, and fungal diseases**

How to manage it:

- Use **deep mulch** (4–6 inches) to keep soil cool and moist
- Install **drip irrigation** or soaker hoses to reduce evaporation
- Provide **partial shade** for young or tender trees during peak heat
- Choose varieties that are **heat-tolerant** but still need some chill hours

Bonus: In Zone 8, well-managed heat = **incredible flavor**, especially for peaches, figs, grapes, and berries.

Mild Winters: Less Risk, Less Reset

Winters in Zone 8 are short and generally mild, with average lows between **10°F and 20°F (–12°C to –6°C)**.

That's good news for:

- Cold-sensitive fruits like **citrus, pomegranates, olives, and loquats**
- Late-ripening varieties that need a longer season
- Reduced risk of bark splitting, root damage, or deep freezes

But it also means:

- Some classic fruits (like apples, cherries, or pears) need **low-chill or hybrid varieties** to flower and fruit properly
- **Pest and disease cycles may not fully reset**, so you need better hygiene and rotation strategies

Solution: Choose **chill-hour-compatible trees**, and **manage orchard hygiene** actively in winter.

Recap – What the Zone 8 Climate Means for Your Orchard

Factor	Impact	Your Advantage
Early spring	Rapid growth, early planting	Start crops sooner and extend harvests
Hot summers	Heat stress, fruit ripening, pests	Flavor boost + longer production window
Mild winters	Limited dormancy, less dieback	Grow tropical and semi-tropical species
Long season	Up to 240 growing days	Succession planting and double cropping

Zone 8 is full of opportunity—but only if you adapt with it.

Don't treat your orchard like it's in the north. Don't fear the heat—**work with it.**

When you understand the rhythm of this zone, you can create a fruit garden that's lush, productive, and nearly year-round.

In the next section, we'll look at which trees and berries thrive best in this environment—and how to **match them to your specific goals and space.**

Let's discover what grows best in your warm, abundant zone.

Subtropical Fruit Trees

USDA Zone 8 opens the door to fruits that colder regions can only dream of. Thanks to **mild winters and a long, hot growing season**, you can grow a rich mix of:

- Classic temperate fruits (like apples and pears)
- Subtropical fruits (like figs, pomegranates, and even some citrus)
- Hardy berries that thrive in heat and produce over an extended season

Let's explore which species and varieties are **perfectly suited for Zone 8**, and how to **combine them for continuous, resilient production.**

Subtropical fruit trees that thrive in your area

These trees love warmth, need minimal chill hours, and reward you with **exotic flavors and abundant yields** when given the right care.

Figs

- **Time to fruit:** 2–3 years
- **Top varieties:** *Celeste, Brown Turkey, LSU Gold, Chicago Hardy*
- Grow in full sun with well-drained soil. Drought-tolerant once established.
- **Harvest:** Late summer to early fall
  Low maintenance and ideal for dry, sunny spots.

Pomegranates (Punica granatum)

- **Time to fruit:** 2–4 years
- **Top varieties:** *Russian 26, Parfianka, Wonderful*
- Tolerates heat and drought; prefers hot summers for full ripening
- **Harvest:** Late summer to fall
  Cold-tolerant down to 10°F with minimal protection.

Loquats (Eriobotrya japonica)

- **Time to fruit:** 3–5 years
- Evergreen tree with early spring fruit
- Sweet, citrus-like flavor; cold-sensitive below 20°F

- **Harvest:** Late winter to early spring

  Needs a protected microclimate (near a south-facing wall).

Citrus (select cold-hardy types only)

- **Time to fruit:** 2–3 years
- **Best bets for Zone 8:**
  - *Satsuma Mandarin*
  - *Meyer Lemon*
  - *Kumquat*
  - *Calamondin*
- Grow in containers or protected spots; may need winter protection
- **Harvest:** Fall to winter

Bring potted citrus indoors during frost events for reliability.

Persimmons (Diospyros spp.)

- **Time to fruit:** 4–6 years
- **Varieties:**
  - *American types* (e.g. *Yates, Meader*) are very hardy
  - *Asian types* (e.g. *Fuyu, Hachiya*) need a warm spot
- **Harvest:** Fall, after first light frost

Beautiful fall color + excellent storage fruit.

Heat-Tolerant and Resilient Berries for Zone 8

Berries love sun—but not all tolerate long heat waves.

These varieties perform well in Zone 8 without daily pampering.

Blackberries

- **Time to fruit:** 1–2 years
- **Top types:** *Ouachita, Natchez, Prime-Ark Freedom*
- Some varieties produce on new canes (everbearing)
- **Harvest:** Summer through early fall

Thornless and productive with minimal care.

Blueberries (Rabbiteye types)

- **Time to fruit:** 2–3 years
- **Top types:** *Climax, Brightwell, Tifblue*
- More heat-tolerant than highbush; needs acidic soil (pH 4.5–5.5)
- **Harvest:** Mid to late summer

Plant at least two varieties for cross-pollination.

Raspberries

- **Time to fruit:** 1–2 years
- **Recommended for Zone 8:**
    o *Dorman Red* (heat-tolerant)
    o *Heritage* (fall-bearing, partial shade preferred)
- **Harvest:** Late spring to early fall

Provide afternoon shade to extend productivity.

Goji Berries (Lycium barbarum)

- **Time to fruit:** 2–3 years
- Thrive in full sun, drought-tolerant once established
- **Harvest:** Late summer

Nutrient-dense and great for hedges or trellises.

<u>Combine and Conquer: Subtropical + Berry Strategy</u>

To get the most from your orchard:

- Mix **early, mid, and late producers** for staggered harvests
- Place subtropical trees in **full sun, warm zones**
- Use berries to **fill gaps** in the season and provide ground-level yields
- Create **guilds**: e.g. figs with comfrey + oregano + pollinator flowers
- Use **microclimates** (walls, slopes, sheltered corners) to expand your species list

Zone 8 is a grower's playground—**more fruit, more flavors, more freedom**. By combining **subtropical fruit trees** with **heat-tolerant berries**, you can create an orchard that delivers **month after month**, with less worry about frost, and more room for creativity.

In the next section, we'll help you manage this abundance—**from watering strategies to disease prevention**, so you can keep everything thriving in the heat.

Summer Care & Water Conservation

Long days, high heat, and sometimes weeks without rain can **stress your trees**, reduce fruit quality, and increase pest problems.

But don't worry—you don't need a complex irrigation system or a daily watering ritual.

With smart planning and a few well-timed actions, you can **conserve water**, protect your trees, and **make the most of summer without wasting a drop**. Let's break it down into what works.

1. Mulch: Your First Line of Defense

Mulch is the **simplest and most effective tool** for protecting roots from heat and evaporation.

How to mulch effectively:

- Use **4–6 inches** of organic mulch (wood chips, shredded leaves, straw)
- Keep a **3–5 inch space** around the trunk to prevent rot
- Replenish mulch **mid-summer** if it breaks down or washes away
- For berry beds, add mulch mats or straw between rows

Result: Cooler soil, fewer weeds, better water retention = stronger trees.

2. Deep Watering, Less Often

Frequent light watering promotes shallow roots—which dry out faster. Instead, aim for **deep, infrequent watering**.

Recommended watering routine for Zone 8:

- Water **2 times per week** for young trees, **1 time/week** for mature trees
- Let water soak to **6–12 inches deep**
- Best time to water: **early morning** (cooler temps, less evaporation)

Use **drip irrigation** or **soaker hoses** to deliver water directly to the roots.

3. Use Shade Strategically

Even sun-loving trees can benefit from a break during the **peak heat of the day**.

How to create beneficial shade:

- Plant low-growing companions (*comfrey, oregano, sweet potato*) at the base of trees
- Use **shade cloth** (30–50% density) for young or sensitive trees
- Trellis fast-growing vines (like pole beans) near exposed areas for temporary shade
- Use white tree paint on trunks to **prevent sunscald**

Especially helpful for: figs, citrus, raspberries, and young stone fruits.

4. Improve Airflow to Reduce Heat Stress and Disease

In humid summers, stagnant air can lead to:

- **Fungal outbreaks**
- **Insect pressure**
- **Leaf scorch**

What to do:

- Prune gently in early summer to open the canopy
- Remove crossing branches and water sprouts
- Thin dense berry patches to allow wind circulation
- Keep rows and tree spacing **open enough for light and breeze**

Airflow = less heat buildup + less disease = healthier fruit.

5. Smart Water Storage and Use

Zone 8 summers can be **unpredictable**—periods of rain may be followed by long dry spells.

Having water ready in advance gives you peace of mind and flexibility.

Simple water-saving solutions:

- **Rain barrels** on gutters or shed roofs
- Use **graywater** (from clean household sources, like rinse water) for ornamental trees
- Add **swales** or shallow trenches to capture stormwater runoff
- Position fruit trees slightly uphill from **mulched retention basins**

In dry climates, water harvesting = self-reliance and sustainability.

Quick Checklist:

- Mulch deeply to insulate roots and hold moisture
- Water early, deeply, and directly at the base
- Provide temporary shade for young trees or tender fruits
- Prune lightly to improve airflow and reduce heat buildup

- Catch and store rainwater for dry weeks

Summer in Zone 8 doesn't have to mean stress, scorched leaves, or cracked fruit.

With the right balance of **shade, water, and airflow,** your orchard can **thrive even during the hottest months.**

In fact, the long summer is your superpower—if you work with it, not against it.

In the next section, we'll help you carry that momentum into the **harvest and fall transition,** with guidance on when and how to pick, clean up, and prepare your trees for the next growing cycle.

Selecting Low-Chill Fruit Varieties

One of the biggest mistakes new growers make in Zone 8 is choosing fruit trees that need more cold than the climate can deliver.

Most temperate fruit trees require a certain number of **chilling hours**—hours between 32°F and 45°F (0°C–7°C)—to break dormancy and set fruit in spring. In Zone 8, these hours typically range from **400 to 800 per year,** depending on location.

If you plant varieties that need **more cold than you get,** here's what happens:

- Trees leaf out late or unevenly

- Flowers are weak or don't form at all

- You get poor or no fruit, year after year

That's why selecting **low-chill varieties** is essential for consistent success in your orchard.

What Are Chilling Hours?

Chilling hours are the **cold period that deciduous fruit trees need during winter** to reset their internal cycle.

Each species—and each variety—has its own requirement.

In Zone 8, you need varieties that require **no more than 800 chilling hours,** and ideally **below 600 hours** for consistent results.

Best Low-Chill Fruit Tree Varieties for Zone 8

Here's a list of reliable performers that thrive with limited chill.

Peaches

- *Flordaprince* – 150 hours, early ripening
- *Tropic Beauty* – 200–300 hours, good flavor
- *Desert Gold* – 300 hours, very early harvest
  Peaches are among the easiest low-chill fruits if pruned annually and protected from frost.

Pears

- *Hood* – 150–300 hours, crisp and juicy
- *Flordahome* – 300–400 hours, fire blight resistant
- *Kieffer* – 350–400 hours, firm texture, great for canning
  Choose soft-flesh or hybrid types; European pears often need more chill.

Apples

- *Anna* – 200–300 hours, excellent flavor, early
- *Dorsett Golden* – 250–300 hours, pairs well with Anna for pollination
- *Ein Shemer* – 300 hours, self-pollinating
  Low-chill apples are ideal for early harvest and mild winters.

Cherries

- *Minnie Royal* – ~300 hours, needs pollinator
- *Royal Lee* – ~300 hours, pollinates Minnie Royal
  Cherries are more difficult, but these two low-chill varieties can succeed with care.

Blueberries (Rabbiteye types)

- *Brightwell, Climax, Premier* – 300–500 hours
  More tolerant of heat and drought than northern highbush types.

Other Low-Chill Trees

- **Figs** (*Celeste, LSU Purple*) – No chill required

- **Pomegranates** (*Parfianka, Russian 26*) – Low chill, very heat-tolerant
- **Persimmons** (*Fuyu, Hachiya*) – Minimal chill, strong producers in Zone 8
- **Citrus** (*Meyer Lemon, Satsuma, Kumquat*) – No chill, protect in frost

Tips for Success with Low-Chill Trees

- **Buy from local or regional nurseries**—they know what works in your exact climate
- **Don't guess** chilling hours—check historical data in your area
- **Mix early, mid, and late-season producers** to spread out your harvest
- **Avoid high-chill "classic" varieties** unless you live in a microclimate that supports them
- **Track bloom and fruit set in your orchard journal**—your own data is gold

In Zone 8, success starts before you plant—**with the right variety.**

Low-chill trees are specially adapted to your climate. They wake up on time, bloom strong, and fruit reliably without fighting nature.

Choosing the right trees now means **less frustration, less guesswork, and more fruit** for years to come.

In the next section, we look at how to manage diseases and parasites naturally and effectively.

Summer Pest & Disease Control, Naturally

In Zone 8, summer is the most active time—not just for your plants, but for **insects, fungi, and bacteria.**

Warm nights, humid mornings, and dense foliage create the perfect conditions for problems to spread quickly if not managed early.

But here's the good news:

You don't need to spray chemicals everywhere.

With the right natural strategies, you can **keep pests and diseases under control** while still protecting your pollinators, your soil, and your long-term yields.

Let's go step-by-step through a natural defense system that works—especially in the heat.

1. Prevention Is Your First (and Best) Strategy

Healthy trees resist problems better. So your first step is to **make your orchard unwelcoming to pests and pathogens.**

What to do:

- **Prune for airflow** – keeps leaves dry and reduces mildew and mold
- **Water at the base** – wet leaves = fungal paradise
- **Clear fallen fruit and leaves** weekly
- **Rotate berries and annuals** if possible
- **Avoid overfeeding with nitrogen**, which creates soft, pest-attracting growth

A clean, balanced orchard is your best pesticide.

2. Organic Sprays That Work (and When to Use Them)

Natural doesn't mean weak—**if you use the right tools at the right time.**

Neem Oil

- Insecticide + antifungal
- Effective against aphids, mites, beetles, and powdery mildew
- Spray early morning or at dusk (never in full sun)
- Apply every 7–10 days if needed

Insecticidal Soap

- Kills soft-bodied insects (aphids, whiteflies, young scale) on contact
- Use on undersides of leaves during infestations

- Repeat weekly if pests persist

Copper Fungicide

- Preventative for leaf spot, fire blight, and bacterial issues
- Use at first signs of disease—**not during flowering**
- Apply only when necessary to avoid copper buildup in soil

Homemade Sprays

- Garlic and chili infusions repel many insects
- Baking soda + water + mild soap helps reduce powdery mildew
- Horsetail (Equisetum) tea strengthens natural plant immunity

Always **test natural sprays on one branch** before applying to the whole plant.

3. Attract the Right Insects (and Let Them Work for You)

Nature gives you allies—use them.

Beneficial insects **hunt pests, pollinate, and protect your trees.**

Encourage these helpers:

- **Ladybugs** – aphids, mites, scale
- **Lacewings** – soft-bodied larvae, whiteflies
- **Parasitic wasps** – caterpillars, borers, beetle larvae
- **Hoverflies** – aphids and scale

How to attract them:

- Plant **dill, fennel, yarrow, calendula, borage, alyssum**
- Let some herbs **go to flower** (basil, mint, oregano)
- Avoid broad-spectrum pesticides, even organic ones

Companion planting = natural pest control that lasts all season.

4. Common Summer Pests and What to Do Naturally

Pest	Signs	Natural Solution
Aphids	Curling leaves, sticky residue	Neem, insecticidal soap, ladybugs

Japanese beetles	Skeletonized leaves	Shake into soapy water, netting, kaolin clay
Spider mites	Yellow spots, fine webbing	Neem, increase humidity, predatory mites
Fruit flies	Larvae in overripe fruit	Remove fallen fruit, use traps
Codling moth	Worms in apples/pears	Use pheromone traps, clean dropped fruit
Powdery mildew	White fuzz on leaves	Baking soda spray, prune for airflow
Fire blight	Blackened, burned-looking tips	Cut infected limbs, copper spray preventively

Tip: Summer Pest Patrol Routine (15 min/week)

- **Walk your orchard** early morning or sunset
- Flip leaves and check undersides
- Look for sticky spots, curling, holes, or discoloration
- Take quick notes in your orchard journal
- Spot early = solve quickly = protect your harvest

Natural Pest Control Toolbox for Zone 8 Growers

- Neem oil or soap spray
- Pruning shears (for air and sanitation)
- Yellow sticky traps or pheromone lures
- Garlic/chili spray or baking soda mix
- Flowering companion plants
- Weekly observation habit

You don't need a perfect orchard—just a responsive one.

In Zone 8, **summer stress is normal**, but disaster isn't.

If you start early, observe often, and respond naturally, you'll stay ahead of the problems—and let nature do the heavy lifting.

Applying Permaculture in Hot Climates
Designing a Self-Sustaining Orchard for Heat, Drought, and Abundance

In hot zones like USDA 8, permaculture isn't just a philosophy—it's a survival strategy.

Long summers, short winters, and unpredictable rainfall mean that every decision—from **plant spacing** to **water use**—has a real impact.

But here's the opportunity:

When done right, **permaculture in hot climates can produce more with less**—less water, less input, and less intervention.

Let's explore how to use nature's logic to design an orchard that's not only productive, but **resilient to heat and stress**.

1. Use Sun Wisely: Work With, Not Against, the Heat

In Zone 8, sunlight is abundant—and sometimes excessive.

The key is to **capture the right amount** and **deflect the rest**.

Strategies:

- Plant heat-sensitive trees (like citrus, young berries) on the **east side of larger trees**
- Use **light-colored mulch** to reflect light and cool the soil
- Position reflective surfaces (like white walls) to extend early sun in cooler months
- Add **climbing vines (grapes, beans)** to provide seasonal shade over walkways or garden edges

Create **microclimates**: small pockets where temperature, wind, and humidity can be moderated for sensitive species.

2. Design for Water Capture and Storage

In a hot climate, every drop counts. Permaculture in Zone 8 means **storing rain, slowing runoff, and keeping water in the soil.**

Techniques:

- Build **swales** (shallow, level ditches) to catch rainwater along slopes
- Use **mulch basins** around trees to trap and sink water where it's needed
- Install **rain barrels** on every roof surface
- Choose **deep-rooted trees** that can access groundwater once established
- Group plants by water needs (this is called "hydrozoning")

Healthy soil holds more water—add organic matter like compost and cover crops regularly.

3. Maximize Biodiversity to Stabilize the Ecosystem

Heat and drought reduce resilience—**biodiversity restores it.**

Include:

- **Native drought-tolerant species** (e.g. elderberry, prickly pear, jujube)
- **Pollinator-friendly plants** like echinacea, lavender, salvia, marigold
- **Insect-repelling herbs** like basil, thyme, oregano
- **Low-growing groundcovers** like sweet potato, creeping thyme, or clover
- **Multiple fruiting seasons** to attract and feed beneficial insects year-round

Every layer of diversity helps balance pests, shade soil, and reduce evaporation.

4. Design with Vertical Layers (Stacking Functions)

Permaculture in hot climates shines when you build **shade, soil, and yield** into every vertical layer.

A typical warm-climate orchard guild:

- **Canopy**: fruit tree (e.g. peach, fig, pomegranate)
- **Understory**: berry bush or dwarf citrus
- **Ground cover**: clover, sweet potato, mulch plants
- **Root layer**: garlic, onions, daikon radish
- **Climbers**: pole beans or grapes up a fence or pergola
- **Mycelial layer**: grow wine cap mushrooms in shady, mulched zones

More layers = more life = more stability, especially under heat stress.

5. Think Cycles, Not Tasks

Permaculture encourages you to **observe patterns**, not just complete checklists.

In hot climates, cycles matter more than fixed schedules:

- Water **based on soil feel and rainfall**, not the calendar
- Prune **when airflow is blocked**, not just in winter
- Feed **when trees are growing** or recovering, not automatically

This approach makes your orchard more adaptive—and you a more intuitive grower.

Quick Summary:

Use shade to protect young trees and preserve soil moisture

- Harvest and store rainwater with swales, basins, and barrels
- Plant in layers to reduce stress and increase yield
- Include native and companion plants for ecosystem balance
- Adjust care to natural cycles—not artificial timelines

In hot climates, **efficiency is everything**.

Permaculture turns your orchard into a system that cools itself, feeds itself, and protects itself—with less work from you.

Whether you have a backyard, a small farm, or a food forest in progress, the principles stay the same:

observe deeply, plant wisely, and design with nature—not against it.

Next, we'll turn all of this into action with your **Zone 8 Annual Care Calendar**—month-by-month strategies to grow fruit successfully all year long.

Annual Orchard Care Calendar

Zone 8 offers an incredibly long growing season—often from **February to November**—but this also means more time for **pests, heat stress, and overgrowth**.

Consistency, observation, and good timing are your best allies.

Let's walk through each phase of the year with smart, seasonal tasks.

Late Winter / Early Spring (February–March)

Prepare for rapid growth and early flowering

Tasks:

- Prune deciduous trees before bud break (apples, pears, peaches)
- Apply dormant oil spray if needed
- Clean up mulch and fallen branches
- Plant bare-root trees and shrubs
- Apply compost or organic soil amendments
- Mulch newly planted trees (leave space around the trunk)

Watering: Begin watering if rainfall is low and the soil is dry at 4–6 inches.

Spring (April–May)

Planting, pest prevention, and early fruit set

Tasks:

- Plant potted trees, berry bushes, and guild companions
- Add or refresh mulch (4–6 inches deep)
- Monitor for aphids, caterpillars, leaf spot, mildew
- Thin fruits if trees are overloaded after bloom
- Fertilize with compost tea, seaweed, or organic blends

- Install trellises for vines or canes if needed

Watering: Water deeply 1–2x per week. Observe leaf color and soil texture.

Early Summer (June)

Heat protection, pest management, and light pruning

Tasks:

- Apply neem oil or insecticidal soap at first sign of pests
- Prune lightly to increase airflow (especially for berries and figs)
- Harvest early berries (e.g., mulberries, raspberries)
- Shade sensitive plants with cloth or vine cover
- Watch for sunburn or cracked fruit—add mulch if soil is hot

Watering: 2–3 deep waterings/week depending on soil and heat level.

Mid to Late Summer (July–August)

Hydration, harvest, and stress reduction

Tasks:

- Continue harvesting blackberries, figs, peaches, plums
- Check for spider mites, beetles, and mildew
- Maintain mulch to reduce evaporation
- Stop nitrogen fertilization by mid-August
- Compost fallen or damaged fruit—don't leave on the ground
- Apply shade where needed for citrus and young trees

Watering: Deep watering 2x per week minimum—more during heat waves.

Early Fall (September)

Late harvesting and soil building

Tasks:

- Harvest apples, late figs, persimmons, pomegranates
- Start fall compost pile
- Sow cover crops (clover, daikon, buckwheat) to enrich soil

- Light pruning if canopy is dense
- Clean orchard floor from fallen fruit to avoid pests

Watering: Adjust based on rain; reduce slightly as temperatures cool.

Late Fall (October–November)

Prepare for dormancy and cold snaps

Tasks:

- Finish harvesting citrus and cold-hardy fruits
- Apply thick winter mulch around tree bases
- Protect young or tropical trees with fleece or frost cloth
- Wrap trunks of young trees to prevent sunscald
- Clean and store tools, drip lines, and hoses

Watering: Water only if the fall is very dry—once every 10–14 days if needed.

Winter (December–January)

Rest, repair, and review

Tasks:

- Plan next year's orchard additions
- Order seeds, trees, or tools
- Prune only if conditions are dry and mild
- Review orchard journal and set new goals
- Attend local workshops or learn more on soil health and companion planting

Watering: Usually not needed unless a winter drought occurs.

Summary Table – USDA Zone 8 Monthly Orchard Care

Month	Focus	Key Tasks
Feb–Mar	Pruning & soil prep	Prune, plant bare root, apply compost

Apr–May	Planting & pest watch	Mulch, fertilize, monitor for pests, thin fruits
June	Airflow & light harvest	Prune, protect from sun, start berry harvest
July–Aug	Hydration & fruit management	Deep water, mulch, pest check, stop nitrogen
Sept	Fall harvest & soil building	Pick late fruit, compost, sow cover crops
Oct–Nov	Cold prep & protection	Mulch, protect trunks, finish harvests
Dec–Jan	Rest & planning	Plan, review journal, light pruning if weather allows

Zone 8 gives you one of the **longest and most productive fruit-growing seasons** available—**if you plan wisely and act with the rhythm of the climate**. This calendar helps you stay consistent, responsive, and efficient—so your orchard gives back **month after month**, with less stress and more satisfaction. Now that your seasonal roadmap is complete, you're ready to manage your orchard with confidence and clarity

Conclusion

Growing fruit trees isn't just about technique—it's about returning to what truly matters: the rhythm of nature, the connection to the earth, and the quiet joy of watching something grow because of your care.

It doesn't matter if your land is large or small, or whether you're starting from scratch or already on your way.

What matters is that you've chosen to begin—to care for a piece of the world and turn it into something nourishing and beautiful.

Every tree you plant is an act of faith in the future.

Every fruit you harvest will be the reward of patience, intention, and love.

This book was written to walk beside you—not to overwhelm you with theory, but to empower you with simple tools and timeless principles. It has shown you how to grow not just an orchard, but a deeper relationship with your land and your way of living.

Now it's your turn:

- Observe, plant, and explore.
- Be gentle with the soil and steady with your hands.
- And most of all, enjoy the process. Because every season—even the slow or imperfect ones—brings something to learn, to taste, and to celebrate.

May your orchard grow strong, healthy, and generous—just like your decision to return to your roots.

Made in the USA
Columbia, SC
23 July 2025

60962296R00059